Can America Compete?

Can America Compete?

ROBERT Z. LAWRENCE

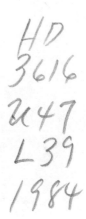
THE BROOKINGS INSTITUTION
Washington, D.C.

Library of Congress Cataloging in Publication data:
Lawrence, Robert Z., 1949–
    Can America Compete?
    Includes bibliographical references and index.
        1. Industry and state—United States. 2. United
    States—Industries. 3. United States—Manufactures.
    4. Industrial productivity—United States. I. Title.
    HD3616.U47L39   1984   338.0973   84-9401
    ISBN 0-8157-5176-1
    ISBN 0-8157-5175-3 (pbk.)

    9 8 7 6 5 4

THE BROOKINGS INSTITUTION is an independent organization devoted to nonpartisan research, education, and publication in economics, government, foreign policy, and the social sciences generally. Its principal purposes are to aid in the development of sound public policies and to promote public understanding of issues of national importance.

The Institution was founded on December 8, 1927, to merge the activities of the Institute for Government Research, founded in 1916, the Institute of Economics, founded in 1922, and the Robert Brookings Graduate School of Economics and Government, founded in 1924.

The Board of Trustees is responsible for the general administration of the Institution, while the immediate direction of the policies, program, and staff is vested in the President, assisted by an advisory committee of the officers and staff. The by-laws of the Institution state: "It is the function of the Trustees to make possible the conduct of scientific research, and publication, under the most favorable conditions, and to safeguard the independence of the research staff in the pursuit of their studies and in the publication of the results of such studies. It is not a part of their function to determine, control, or influence the conduct of particular investigations or the conclusions reached."

The President bears final responsibility for the decision to publish a manuscript as a Brookings book. In reaching his judgment on the competence, accuracy, and objectivity of each study, the President is advised by the director of the appropriate research program and weighs the views of a panel of expert outside readers who report to him in confidence on the quality of the work. Publication of a work signifies that it is deemed a competent treatment worthy of public consideration but does not imply endorsement of conclusions or recommendations.

The Institution maintains its position of neutrality on issues of public policy in order to safeguard the intellectual freedom of the staff. Hence interpretations or conclusions in Brookings publications should be understood to be solely those of the authors and should not be attributed to the Institution, to its trustees, officers, or other staff members, or to the organizations that support its research.

For Nicole

Foreword

Is America deindustrializing? Are we becoming "a nation of hamburger stands"? Is the rest of the world out-competing American industry? In this study, Robert Z. Lawrence analyzes the sources of structural change in U.S. manufacturing, compares U.S. industrial performance with that of other major industrial countries, estimates the effects of exchange rates on U.S. manufacturing, and draws conclusions for policy. His findings challenge many widely held views.

Lawrence finds that America is not deindustrializing. In the 1970s neither international trade nor a failure to invest in industrial plant and equipment can be blamed for the growth slowdown of the manufacturing sector. Particularly from 1973 to 1980, trade had a positive effect on U.S. manufacturing employment, with benefits to many U.S. industries. During this same period, rates of capital formation in U.S. manufacturing exceeded their historical averages and matched or exceeded those of other industrial countries. Between 1980 and 1983 the changes that occurred in U.S. manufacturing employment and in trade flows were the predictable consequences of recession and recovery and the strong dollar.

Lawrence's analysis leads him to stress the crucial role of U.S. macroeconomic policies in improving the performance of American firms in international trade. Reductions in the government deficit, he believes, are the key to lowering the trade deficit. In the last part of his study he evaluates proposals for new U.S. industrial policies and offers some suggestions for policies to facilitate structural change.

The research on which this book is based was financed in part by a grant from the Alex C. Walker Educational and Charitable Foundation. For research assistance, the author thanks Kenneth D. Boese, Paula DeMasi, and Edward Gardener, and for computational assistance, the staff of the Brookings Social Science Computation Center. He is grateful for comments and suggestions from Barry P. Bosworth, Edward R.

Denison, Carol Heim, Gary C. Hufbauer, Lawrence B. Krause, Joseph A. Pechman, George L. Perry, Alice M. Rivlin, Charles L. Schultze, and Robert M. Stern. The author also benefited from comments by participants at the Conference on the Political Economy of Inflation and Unemployment held at Williams College, October 1982; at the April 1983 meeting of the Brookings Panel on Economic Activity; and at the August 1983 Symposium on Industrial Change and Public Policy sponsored by the Federal Reserve Bank of Kansas City in Jackson Hole, Wyoming. Chapter 3 of this book is based in part on a paper originally presented before the Brookings Panel in April 1983 and first published in *Brookings Papers on Economic Activity, 1:1983*. The author also thanks Charlotte Kaiser, Evelyn M. E. Taylor, and Anita G. Whitlock for secretarial assistance. Karen J. Wirt edited the manuscript, Penelope Schmitt verified its factual content, Nancy Snyder served as proofreader, and Ward & Silvan prepared the index.

The views expressed here are those of the author and should not be ascribed to the Alex C. Walker Foundation or to the officers, trustees, or staff members of the Brookings Institution.

BRUCE K. MACLAURY
President

March 1984
Washington, D.C.

Contents

Figures

CHAPTER ONE

A Nation of Hamburger Stands?

FOR THE FIRST TIME in postwar history, employment in U.S. manufacturing fell for three consecutive years; between 1979 and 1982 the number of workers in U.S. manufacturing declined 10.4 percent, the largest drop since the wartime economy demobilized between 1943 and 1946. The slump was also unusual because international trade was a significant contributing factor: normally the volume of imports of manufactured goods falls steeply in a recession—yet from 1980 to 1982, it rose by 8.3 percent; normally U.S. manufactured exports reflect growth in export markets abroad—yet despite a 5.3 percent rise in these markets from 1980 to 1982, the volume of U.S. manufactured exports dropped 17.5 percent.

Many observers believe the erosion of U.S. industrial employment reflects more than transitory business-cycle and exchange-rate fluctuations. They see a secular decline in the U.S. industrial base that stems from deep-rooted structural difficulties. U.S. producers are blamed for failing to produce quality goods. Managers are perceived as myopic: they care only about short-term profits and have failed to invest in new equipment and research and development. Workers seem to lack discipline and are shackled by work rules. And labor and management consider each other as adversaries. Others accuse the U.S. government. One group blames it for excessive interference—restrictive regulatory practices that have raised production costs; faulty tax rules that have discouraged investment, saving, and innovation; and trade protection that has slowed adjustment to international competition. Others blame government negligence. They feel that the United States has failed to plan and coordinate its industrial evolution and that it ought to have policies to promote industries with potential and to assist those in decline. Finally, there is also the more fatalistic view of the decline in U.S. manufacturing as the inevitable result of the rapid international diffusion of U.S. technology.

1

While it is argued that particular U.S. deficiencies have become worse over time, changes in the environment are also thought to have made U.S. structural flaws increasingly costly. As long as competition was primarily domestic, U.S. weaknesses were obscured. As global trade expanded, however, U.S. firms faced foreign competitors staffed with superior work forces and managers and backed by favorable government policies. In the developing countries advances in automation have allowed producers to equip their low-wage work forces with the most modern machinery and to become highly competitive in consumer electronics, shipbuilding, steel, textiles, and consumer goods. In the developed countries international technological diffusion, rapid growth in capital formation, and increased innovation have enabled producers to compete successfully with U.S. producers in high-technology products.

The perceived effect of international competition has now grown to such an extent that it is frequently cited as the major source of structural change in the U.S. economy and the primary reason for the declining share of manufacturing in U.S. employment. This shift of U.S. production away from manufacturing is viewed with some alarm, both because manufacturing activity is considered intrinsically desirable and because of the adjustment costs associated with the shift. Manufacturing is seen as the fulcrum of a modern economy, an important source of high-wage jobs and employment, the major locus of productivity growth, the center of vital regional economies, and a crucial element for national defense. The turbulence associated with the change now under way in U.S. industry is seen as costly and disruptive.

Policymakers differ in their strategies for restoring U.S. industrial competitiveness, but on both the right and the left there is agreement that the problems are structural and that they originate in the international economy. The Reagan administration views the problem as a comparative failure of U.S. investment and, accordingly, has implemented new tax policies as a remedy. Others consider the decline in U.S. competitiveness in manufacturing to be mainly the result of the industrial and trade policies adopted by other nations. As proponents of this view contend, without similar U.S. policies, the United States will eventually become an economy specializing in farm products and services—"a nation of hamburger stands."

Yet, although the role of the deficiencies in U.S. policies and practices in retarding U.S. productivity growth over the past decade remains unclear, the links among these deficiencies, U.S. trade performance, and changes in U.S. economic structure have not been convincingly demonstrated.

There are several implicit assumptions in the current discussion about U.S. industrial performance that I show in this book to be inappropriate. First, policy discussion often presumes that rapid growth of productivity will increase the share of resources devoted to an activity and that higher productivity will create jobs. The existence of elastic demand is assumed. As the experience of U.S. agriculture has demonstrated, however, rapid growth of productivity in the face of limited markets may have the opposite effect. Indeed, as I will indicate, the declining employment in Japanese manufacturing in the 1970s and the contrasting rise in U.S. employment highlight the possibility that manufacturing productivity and employment could in some cases be negatively related.

Second, a decline in international technological lead in a particular area is argued to reduce the resources devoted to that activity. Proponents of that argument assume that an erosion in absolute advantage will lead to an erosion in *comparative* advantage. Yet, as I show below, even though foreign productive capabilities are converging with those of the United States, the U.S. *comparative* advantage in high technology products has actually increased.[1]

Third, the current discussion presumes that the U.S. trade balance can decline indefinitely. It ignores the automatic adjustment mechanisms that tend to keep the trade balance in goods and services within fairly narrow bounds. An increase in imports eventually leads to an increase in exports. When global demand shifts away from U.S. products, it creates an excess supply of American goods and an excess demand for foreign goods. Since the relative price of U.S. goods may have to fall to restore the trade balance, resources devoted to export production will have to *increase,* for a decline in the terms of trade entails providing more exports for any given volume of imports.

Fourth, productivity growth in U.S. manufacturing has been slower than it has for its industrial competitors, and this is automatically

---

1. It is a basic tenet of trade theory that nations specialize in the production of goods in which they have comparative advantage. Even if, for example, the U.S. lead erodes in both automobiles and computers but computers suffer relatively less, the United States would increase its specialization in computers—that is, the U.S. comparative advantage in computers (over automobiles) would increase. See, for example, Paul A. Samuelson, *Economics,* 11th ed. (McGraw-Hill, 1976), pp. 670–740.

presumed to have an adverse effect on competitiveness in international trade. But international buyers compare prices in a common currency, and the rate of productivity growth is just one element in the determination of price. If more rapid growth of productivity is reflected in higher wages and profits, production costs may remain unchanged. Even superior domestic price performance may be offset by changes in exchange rates. Indeed, as I argue below, the real devaluations of the dollar more than offset the impact of the slower rate of growth of U.S. productivity in the 1970s, thereby contributing to the growth in manufacturing employment over the period.

Finally, international trade is neither the sole nor the most important source of structural change. As I demonstrate, in many cases trade has simply reinforced the effects of demand and technological change. At least five factors have had important effects on the U.S. industrial base: (1) the share of manufactured products in consumer spending has declined secularly because of the pattern of demand associated with rising U.S. income levels; (2) because the demand for manufactured goods is highly sensitive to the total growth rate of GNP, manufacturing production has been slowed disproportionately by the sluggish overall economic growth in the global economy since 1973; (3) some long-run decline in the share of manufacturing in total employment reflects the relatively more rapid productivity growth in this sector; (4) shifts in the pattern of U.S. international specialization have arisen from changes in comparative advantage that, in turn, result from changes in relative factor endowments and production capabilities associated with foreign economic growth and policies; and (5) short-run changes in U.S. international competitiveness have come from changes in exchange rates and cyclical conditions, both at home and abroad.

The appropriate choice of policy depends crucially on the relative impacts of these various factors on current U.S. industrial performance. If the slow rate of U.S. industrial employment growth is the inevitable result of technological change, demand patterns associated with the stage of U.S. economic development, changes in international comparative advantage, or the post-1973 world economic malaise, policies to assist in the allocation of U.S. resources *away* from industry may be required. If inadequate or flagging expenditures on industrial capital formation, R&D, or both are the reason for the slow rate of growth, policies to shift resources *toward* manufacturing may be required. If foreign trade and industrial policies are the reason, the United States may try to change the trading system or its own behavior within it. If exchange rate changes are important, factors such as the monetary-fiscal mix of policy or exchange rate intervention policies may merit attention. If transitory cyclical forces are the cause, there may not be a need for a new industrial policy, but rather for a change in macroeconomic policies or an acknowledgment that the slump brought about by current policies is the unavoidable cost of reducing inflation.

Given the radical changes in the world economy after 1973, the period from 1973 to 1980 is the most relevant sample for current policy discussions. The data for this period measure performance in a new international environment marked by stagnation, volatile exchange rates, surging competition from Japan and the newly industrializing countries, and increasing government intervention in trade. It is alleged that during this period foreign industrial policies damaged the U.S. manufacturing base. The 1973–80 data also allow a comparison of U.S. industrial performance with that of other major industrial countries in a period during which comparative performance was less heavily influenced by relative stages of development. The data also omit the effects of the major dollar appreciations and the recessions that occurred from 1980 to 1982.

Observations for the 1973–80 period, however, may be unduly influenced by the different cyclical positions that prevailed in the end-point years. Because capacity utilization in manufacturing was similar in 1970 and 1980, U.S. data for the entire decade are used to provide a second, cyclically neutral, measure of structural changes.[2] But observations for 1970–80 are still influenced by changes in the real exchange rate of the dollar in these years. As measured by the International Monetary Fund, relative U.S. export prices for manufactured goods were 13.5 percent lower in 1980 than in 1970. When evaluating the results, therefore, it should be kept in mind that the U.S. trade performance during the 1970s depended in part upon this price-adjustment process.

Summary and Conclusions of the Study

This examination of the performance of U.S. manufacturing indicates that, contrary to recent fears, America is not deindustrializing. Although

2. Capacity utilization in U.S. manufacturing, measured by the index of the Federal Reserve Board, was 79.3 percent in 1970 and 79.1 percent in 1980.

the *share* of manufacturing in the economy has declined, the manufacturing sector continues to grow. Chapter 2 compares U.S. manufacturing performance during the past decade with its postwar record. Between 1950 and 1973 the output of manufactured goods grew as fast as GNP. But because productivity growth was more rapid in manufacturing than in the rest of the economy, the share of total U.S. employment, capital, and spending on research and development in manufacturing declined. The demand for manufactured goods is very sensitive to the growth rate of the overall economy. If GNP grows above its long-run trend, manufacturing growth will outstrip it; if GNP grows below its long-run trend, manufacturing growth will lag behind. Thus when GNP growth declined between 1973 and 1980, U.S. manufacturing output growth fell—but by no more than the predictable amount. Nonetheless, over this period the rate of capital formation and R&D spending in manufacturing actually accelerated. The share of manufacturing in total employment fell rapidly, partly because GNP grew slowly and partly because labor productivity growth in manufacturing fell less than it did in the rest of the economy.

The finding that capital formation and R&D spending in manufacturing have accelerated should give pause to those who believe that channeling additional capital toward U.S. manufacturing is an appropriate remedy for America's industrial problems. Evidence points instead to the important role of aggregate demand in constraining manufacturing growth. Resuming growth will stimulate output in manufacturing, and reindustrialization will occur automatically. In the absence of demand for particular products, however, resources should be directed *away* from activities in which they are no longer needed.

The manufacturing slump since 1973 is a worldwide phenomenon. The increase in U.S. manufacturing output since 1973 has been about the same as the average of all industrial countries. Between 1973 and 1980, the capital stock in manufacturing grew more rapidly in the United States than it did in Germany, France, Sweden, and the United Kingdom; and real R&D spending increased as rapidly in U.S. manufacturing as in other major industrial countries. Between 1975 and 1980 the capital stocks in U.S. and Japanese manufacturing grew at similar rates. Although employment in U.S. manufacturing grew modestly, in other major industrial countries it declined, with the exception of small increases in Canada and Italy. In virtually every major industry, employment in the United States grew faster than that in Japan. Although

U.S. labor productivity growth was not as rapid as productivity growth in other industrial countries, U.S. productivity levels in manufacturing and the U.S. share of R&D spending in value added for manufacturing remain the highest in the world. Compared with its postwar track record, between 1973 and 1980 the U.S. manufacturing sector fared relatively better than its counterparts in other industrial countries. This might have been expected given that other countries have exhausted the relative gains of catching up—accomplished by adopting U.S. techniques. The superior performance of the U.S. manufacturing sector may also be ascribed to its greater flexibility in a period marked by external shocks. In particular, U.S. real wage growth has been more adaptable and U.S. labor more mobile. Although American investment flows have shifted toward manufacturing, in the manufacturing sectors of Europe and Japan the share of total investment allocated to manufacturing has declined significantly. Profit rates in manufacturing have fallen considerably less in the United States than they have in Europe.

Although the historical relationship between U.S. manufacturing and GNP has not changed noticeably, in Europe manufacturing production is considerably lower than would have been expected.

The United States has been comparatively successful in shifting its workers from low-growth industries to industries with high growth potential. The share of manufacturing employment in high-technology industries has increased more rapidly in the United States than in Germany or Japan. And the share of employment in labor-intensive manufacturing has declined more rapidly in the United States than in Japan.

Chapter 3 examines the influence of international trade on the U.S. manufacturing sector and reveals a number of findings. Between 1970 and 1980 the volume of U.S. manufactured exports and imports increased—by 101 percent and 72 percent, respectively. Between 1973 and 1980 the trade balance in manufactured goods increased by $18.3 billion; the postwar decline in the U.S. share of world trade in manufactured goods was arrested; and foreign trade provided a net addition to output and jobs in U.S. manufacturing.

U.S. manufacturers, aided only by changes in the exchange rate, were able to compete successfully in an environment characterized by emerging competition from developing countries and Japan and by growing government intervention and protection in Europe.

From 1980 to 1982 the U.S. manufactured goods trade balance declined. This was not the result of a sudden erosion in U.S. international competitiveness brought about by foreign industrial and trade policies. Rather, as the econometric evidence provided in chapter 3 indicates, the decline should have been predictable given previous trends and levels of economic activity and patterns of relative prices.

Changes in the real exchange rate are therefore effective in moving the current account toward an equilibrium that is determined by expenditure patterns. In 1970 and 1980 the current account was a similar percentage of GNP. This stability was accomplished in part by growth in the manufactured goods trade balance because of real devaluation. In the 1980s the shift toward large full-employment government deficits, unmatched by lower private absorption, entails a current account deficit as foreign savings help finance the government deficit. Part of this deficit occurs as a manufactured goods trade deficit achieved through real appreciation. The evidence does not indicate that major changes in U.S. industrial and trade policies are required to maintain external equilibrium. Given a continuation of trends in U.S. and foreign trade policies and growth patterns and the absence of relative price changes, the U.S. trade balance in manufactured goods should register very small annual declines. If required for overall external equilibrium, such declines could be offset by minor improvements in relative U.S. prices.

Despite the weakness in U.S. trade performance, U.S. manufacturing output and employment between 1979 and 1983 have conformed with their historical patterns given overall growth of the economy. This performance by the manufacturing sector suggests that the rise in defense procurement and the strong growth in domestic investment have offset the negative effect of foreign trade.

Chapter 4 takes a close look at the structural change in the U.S. manufacturing sector. The degree of structural change in the 1970s in manufacturing employment was no greater than it was in the 1960s, and considerably less than in the 1950s. The dispersion in employment growth rates across industries in manufacturing in the 1960s and 1970s was remarkably similar. Thus the recent rise in manufacturing unemployment is principally related to the slow overall growth in employment rather than to an increase in structural change at any given growth rate.

The chapter next considers the sources of the structural change that has taken place. Between 1973 and 1980, in thirty-eight of the fifty-two U.S. industries in the manufacturing sector, trade made a positive contribution to employment. Changes in domestic consumption were a far more important cause of structural change than changes in international trade. The perception that foreign competition has been the main source of an absolute decline in the U.S. industrial base stems from trade reinforcing the effects of domestic growth. The U.S. comparative advantage in products of unskilled labor and standardized capital-intensive products has been declining secularly. And, because of slow domestic economic growth, the home market for those products has not expanded rapidly. But the U.S. comparative advantage in high-technology products has strengthened, and growth in the demand for such products has been relatively more rapid in a climate of stagnation.

Chapter 4 also investigates the automobile and steel industries. During the 1970s as a whole the automobile industry was virtually the only one in the U.S. economy in which jobs lost due to trade exceeded jobs gained because of domestic demand. Nonetheless, although atypical, the automobile industry's experience has dominated the headlines. In the period since the 1979 oil shock the U.S. demand has shifted toward small cars. As a result, foreign trade in general and Japanese imports in particular have had a negative effect on U.S. automotive employment. During this period, however, the overall slump in domestic automobile sales has been considerably more important than trade. The picture is much the same in the steel industry. During 1980 to 1982, employment in steel fell sharply; the major reason for this decline was the change in domestic consumption. Thus, despite the prominence given to imports and Japanese competition, imports of steel contributed much less to the decline in steel employment. Because steel is used as an intermediate input, the indirect effects of manufacturing trade in general contributed as much to the decrease in steel employment as actual imports and exports of steel.

Attention has been focused in recent years on the worker dislocation that has accompanied the declines in automobile and steel employment and the gains in the computer industry. However, this employment transition is not representative of the more substantial employment shifts from basic to high-technology industries. Judged by demographic and education characteristics, most workers formerly employed in low-technology industries could be employed in industries with high technology. The latter industries have a geographic distribution that is similar to the rest of manufacturing, and these industries provide similar shares of jobs paying close to median wages. If the U.S. economy could sustain growth at long-run trend levels, industrial shifts due to structural change would not result in significant dislocation.

As a result of the recessions in 1980 and 1982, U.S. employment in both high technology and basic industry was considerably below its long-run trend in 1983. For the next four or five years, provided growth can be sustained, significant increases in employment in both high- and low-technology industries can be anticipated.

The second part of the book surveys policy options to address some of the problems outlined above. Slow overall growth in the economy and a strong currency appear to be the dominant reasons for the adjustment problems facing U.S. manufacturing. Macroeconomic policies contribute significantly to ameliorating these difficulties. If economic growth is sustained, job creation and investment in manufacturing will occur automatically. In the absence of demand, it is wasteful to allocate labor and capital toward manufacturing production.

The current mix of monetary and fiscal policies is inadequate and should be altered. Fiscal policies should be tighter; monetary policies should be easier. The long-run budget deficit should be reduced by decreasing expenditures and increasing taxes (in a manner that does not discourage investment). Monetary policies could then be relatively more expansionary. This policy mix would weaken the dollar, thereby improving the competitiveness of all U.S. firms engaging in international trade. It would also lower real interest rates and stimulate investment, and thereby provide a further boost to manufacturing production.

Even if macroeconomic policy is improved, however, structural policies have a role to play in facilitating adjustment and economic performance. The United States has always had such policies; the key issue is not whether we should have them, but rather how they can be made more effective.

Chapter 5 considers proposals recommending that the United States adopt explicitly selective industrial policies. These proposals suggest that the government should determine a satisfactory industrial structure, perhaps with the assistance of a tripartite committee of business, labor, and management. It should then use a combination of trade policies, an industrial development bank, regulatory policies, and other measures to shift resources in a direction deemed desirable.

In the absence of a change in macroeconomic policies, selective industrial policies may change the composition of the trade balance and employment but are unlikely to affect their aggregate levels. The debate about selective industrial policies is therefore not about how to reduce the trade deficit or increase employment, but about how best to allocate resources.

The empirical case for industrial policies has not been well established. The evidence does not suggest that the decline in U.S. manufacturing productivity growth could have been avoided with a different allocation of resources across U.S. manufacturing sectors. Nor has the United States been sluggish in shifting labor and capital toward high-technology industries. The notion that U.S. capital markets are systematically shortsighted is not supported by empirical tests. Nor is there convincing evidence to show that foreign success is due to superior industrial policies.

Because the data from the 1970s indicate that real exchange rates can maintain equilibrium in the U.S. external accounts, America need not suffer an erosion in the industrial base if it fails to adopt selective industrial policies. The real choice is between relying primarily on market forces to allocate resources or relying on selective industrial policies. Programs that support particular industries, basic or high technology, will divert resources from other sectors of the economy. To determine if such policies could improve the productivity and adjustment of U.S. manufacturing it is necessary to analyze the criteria by which resources would be allocated. Some proponents of industrial policy avoid offering precise criteria by which such policies would appraise projects and sectoral programs. To support these proposals requires placing faith in the superior judgment of officials who carry out such programs. Others have suggested favoring "linkage" industries, industries with high average value added per worker, those favored by foreign targeting, and those able to become competitive in the future. These criteria are likely to be inefficient. Simply because an industry may become internationally competitive does not imply that the efficient way to achieve a given level of trade balance is to promote it. Because an industry has high average value added per worker does not mean that society's living standards will be raised if it expands. Because an industry provides inputs for other industries does not imply there are gains, not captured by producers in that industry, that justify additional social support. And because industries abroad receive government support it does not follow that the U.S. government should provide similar assistance to such industries in the United States. Asking a government board to determine which industries are really needed is the wrong approach.

The real issue is not whether industry A or B is needed, but how large it should be. That marginal decision is one that a central committee is ill-equipped to make.

Another reason why selective industrial policies are inadvisable is that industries are not likely to be appropriate units for policy. Because industries are diverse, aid to an entire industry will inevitably assist many that do not merit support. Objectives such as meeting national defense needs, redistributing income, promoting regional development, and so on can all be achieved by more precise policies. Government support organized at the industry level invariably leads to cartelization and strengthens existing participants at the expense of new entrants.

As a means of subsidizing industries, a government development bank is often suggested as part of the selective industrial policies, but the case for it is particularly weak. If a government investment bank allocated credit to projects offering the highest rates of return, it would simply supplant activity in the private sector. If it did not allocate resources by this criterion, it would waste resources. U.S. capital markets are the world's most highly developed. Firms with growth potential *have* been able to raise substantial amounts of capital. Alleged failures to invest in certain industries may not be failures at all.

A move toward greater government participation in resource allocation is thus unlikely to enhance efficiency given the U.S. political system and administrative traditions. Without a broad national consensus about the necessity for such programs, there can be no continuity in their implementation. Some proponents of selective industrial policies believe that the conditional provision of government aid and trade protection could speed up the pace of domestic adjustment. But it is questionable whether the government has the knowledge and monitoring capabilities to set such conditions. It is also questionable whether government aid could be confined to troubled industries that provide a plan to restore their international competitiveness. Previous efforts to aid depressed regions and cities have been diffused into relatively ineffective programs with numerous recipients receiving token assistance.

Chapter 6 offers some concrete suggestions for improving U.S. structural policies, including the following.

The United States should neither ignore unfair practices abroad nor attempt to match them. It should follow a strategy that maximizes U.S. national welfare. Existing trade laws that provide for offsetting duties in the face of foreign subsidies and unfair practices, but only if the domestic industry can prove injury, are an appropriate compromise between the benefits that accrue to consumers and the costs incurred by producers. Strategic behavior is required to deal with subsidies on exports competing with U.S. products in third world markets and to open up foreign markets through bilateral and multilateral negotiation.

The Reagan administration has yielded to political pressures and provided several major U.S. industries with increased protection. Industries currently protected by nontariff barriers and industries seeking safeguard protection in the future should be aided by self-liquidating tariffs. An improved program to provide trade adjustment assistance should be used as an alternative to protection and as an inducement to industries to avoid circumventing appropriate channels for obtaining relief from international competition. This program would compensate displaced individuals for some proportion of lost income without removing the incentive to find new work. Chapter 6 also argues that trade protection should not be used to preserve industries needed for national defense. Explicit support through the defense budget would be more efficient.

As this study demonstrates, present U.S. structural programs need to be clarified. A new government analytical agency could contribute toward this objective by quantifying the effects of existing programs and policies on resource allocation among industries. The United States also needs new structural programs to address recognized cases of market failure rather than a policy of selecting specific firms and industries for support. There should be increased direct government financing of basic and generic R&D in areas in which the difficulties of appropriating knowledge lead to too little private investment. If private firms are prevented from collaboration, from a social standpoint research efforts could be wastefully duplicated. Removal of government rules that prevent cooperative research ventures should be considered. Another factor is market failure to provide sufficient opportunities for borrowing so that individuals can develop new skills and improve their level of education. A government program that provides loans to finance education and retraining should be considered. These loans should be offered at market interest rates and be collected by the Internal Revenue Service. The existing U.S. tax system arbitrarily distorts investment decisions across sectors of the economy. A more neutral investment tax code should be implemented. Finally, antitrust laws should be revised to reflect new international realities. In particular, provided the U.S. market is not shielded by quota protection, the global market should be used in measuring market concentration.

The book ends with a cautionary note. Attitudes of management and labor will be influenced by the environment. Some features of U.S. industrial behavior—the emphasis on short-term profits and the preservation of flexibility—may be desirable characteristics in an uncertain world. Policy should have as its objective the establishment of an overall environment of sustained growth in which success depends on performance in the marketplace, not on government assistance.

U.S. Manufacturing
and Structural Change

CHAPTER TWO

Is America Deindustrializing?

THE CONTENTION that declining U.S. international competitiveness has induced the deindustrialization of America in the 1970s is incorrect on two counts: in the most relevant sense, the United States did not undergo a deindustrialization; and from 1973 to 1980 the net impact of international competition on the overall size of the U.S. manufacturing sector was small and positive. Between 1980 and 1982 American industrial growth was weak, but this was the predictable result of recession and the strong dollar. To determine whether U.S. manufacturing performance has recently deviated from its historical record, an analysis must focus on the 1970s.

The term *deindustrialization* requires some elaboration for the purposes of this discussion. For example, to what industries does the term refer? Does it include the construction and mining sectors or refer more narrowly, as I interpret it here (partly for reasons of data availability), to the manufacturing sector alone? Does deindustrialization refer to a drop in the output of industry, or to the inputs (such as capital or labor) devoted to industry? Does the term refer to an absolute decline in the volume of output from (or input to) manufacturing, or simply a relative decline in the growth of manufacturing output (input) as compared to output (input) of the rest of the economy?

Because industrial policy is generally designed to facilitate adjustment to changes in industry, absolute deindustrialization with respect to factors of production is probably the most relevant of the current policy concerns about the manufacturing sector as a whole. While a declining share of output or employment could change the relative power of industrial workers or the character of a society, an absolute decline in industrial employment entails much greater adjustment difficulties. Absolute deindustrialization at rates in excess of the normal voluntary quits by workers and the depreciation of capital requires reallocation of workers and capital to alternative sectors in the economy, with all the

17

Table 2-1. *Size and Share of the U.S. Manufacturing Sector, Selected Years, 1950–82*

Billions of 1972 dollars unless otherwise specified

Year	Gross national product	Value added	Employment (millions)[a]	Net capital[b]	Manufacturing share (percent)			
					Real GNP	Spending[c]	Employment	Capital
1950	535	131	15.2	n.a.	24.5	29.2	35.9	n.a.
1960	737	172	16.8	140.4	23.3	28.4	31.0	25.8
1965	939	237	18.1	158.1	25.5	28.6	29.7	23.8
1970	1,086	261	19.4	202.2	24.0	25.4	27.3	23.5
1973	1,255	325	20.2	215.3	25.9	24.5	26.2	22.2
1975	1,232	290	18.3	232.7	23.5	23.1	23.8	22.5
1979	1,479	367	21.0	275.1	24.8	23.3	23.4	23.2
1980	1,474	351	20.3	293.6	23.7	22.1	22.4	23.9
1981	1,503	359	20.2	311.8	23.7	21.9	22.1	24.6
1982	1,477	338	18.9	n.a.	22.9	20.7	21.1	n.a.

Sources: U.S. Department of Commerce, Bureau of Economic Analysis, *The National Income and Product Accounts of the United States, 1929–74 Statistical Tables*, a supplement to the *Survey of Current Business* (Government Printing Office, 1977), and subsequent reports; U.S. Bureau of Labor Statistics, *Employment and Earnings*, vol. 18 (March 1972); U.S. Bureau of the Census, *Statistical Abstract of the United States, 1981* (GPO, 1982), p. 562; and *Survey of Current Business*, vol. 62 (October 1982).

n.a. Not available.

a. Number of employees on nonagricultural payrolls.

b. Net fixed nonresidential capital stock.

c. Ratio of value added in manufacturing to GNP, both in current dollars.

costs associated with such movements. Relative deindustrialization, however, is far less costly to accomplish, for it may entail simply devoting fewer resources to manufacturing in the future.[1]

U.S. Manufacturing in Historical Perspective

As indicated in table 2-1, these distinctions are relevant for characterizing U.S. deindustrialization: measured by the size of its manufacturing labor force, capital stock, and output growth, the United States did not experience absolute deindustrialization over either the 1950–73 period or the 1973–80 period. Employment in U.S. manufacturing rose from 15.2 million in 1950 to 16.8 million in 1960, to 19.4 million in 1970, 20.2 million in 1973, and 20.3 million in 1980.[2] The net capital stock in

1. As I show below, absolute declines of employment in individual industries may be accompanied by considerable adjustment difficulties, even when offset by employment gains in other manufacturing industries.

2. By contrast, employment in U.S. agriculture has undergone an absolute decline—from 8.6 million in 1945 to 3.3 million in 1980.

manufacturing grew at an annual rate of 3.3 percent from 1960 to 1973 and 4.5 percent between 1973 and 1980.[3] Value added in manufacturing increased at an annual rate of 5.0 percent between 1960 and 1973 and 1.1 percent from 1973 to 1980. During the 1970s there was in addition a much publicized decline in the growth of total real expenditures on R&D.[4] Real R&D spending increased 3.1 percent a year from 1960 to 1973, but fell to a 2.5 percent annual growth rate from 1973 to 1980. This decline does not reflect a similar drop in real R&D spending in U.S. industry, however. Between 1960 and 1972 spending in manufacturing grew 2.1 percent a year. From 1972 to 1979 (the latest data available), it accelerated to 2.4 percent. A similar pattern is evident in industry hirings. While the number of scientists and engineers employed in industry R&D grew at 1.2 percent between 1961 and 1973, from 1973 to 1980 growth averaged 3.8 percent a year.[5]

Shares as Indicators

Judged by the output share of goods, the United States could not be characterized as a service economy in 1980 any more than it was in 1960. In 1960, 1973, and 1980 the ratio of goods to the gross national product measured in 1972 dollars was 45.6, 45.6, and 45.3 percent, respectively.[6] Similarly, the share of value added in manufacturing (in 1972 dollars) was actually somewhat higher in 1973 than it was in 1950. Nonetheless, from 1950 to 1973 the *shares* of expenditure, employment, capital stock, and R&D devoted to the manufacturing sector declined. Factors on both the demand and the supply side account for the diminishing share of manufacturing. As U.S. incomes have risen, Americans have allocated increasing proportions of their incomes to items in the service sector

3. The gross capital stock grew at an annual rate of 3.1 percent between 1960 and 1973 and 3.8 percent between 1973 and 1980. See U.S. Department of Commerce, Bureau of the Census, *Statistical Abstract of the United States, 1980* (Government Printing Office, 1980), and *Statistical Abstract of the United States, 1982–83* (GPO, 1982).
4. The decline in growth of R&D spending as a share of GNP in the United States was a reflection of the very slow increase in R&D financed by the government. Civilian R&D grew from 1.2 percent of the gross national product in 1961 to 1.43 percent in 1973 and 1.63 percent in 1980. See National Science Foundation, *Science Indicators, 1980* (GPO, 1981), appendix table 1-4.
5. Ibid.
6. *Economic Report of the President, February 1984*, table B-7, p. 229.

such as government services, education, medical care, finance, and real estate services. At the same time, productivity in manufacturing has increased more rapidly than elsewhere in the economy. Although the more rapid growth in manufacturing productivity has resulted in slower price increases in that sector, the demand stimulated by the relative decline of prices of manufactured goods has not been sufficient to offset the fall in the share of resources devoted to manufacturing.[7] As a result, overall real industrial output has risen about as rapidly as GNP, but, other things being equal, the share of employment and capital in manufactured goods has declined.[8]

From 1973 to 1980 there was a marked acceleration in the rate at which the share of manufacturing in output and employment declined. But this should have been expected, given the slow overall growth in GNP and the fact that labor productivity growth (output per worker-hour) fell less in manufacturing than in the rest of the economy. The demand for manufacturing output is particularly sensitive to fluctuations in income. The demand for goods, particularly durable goods, is inherently more sensitive to short-run income fluctuations than the demand for services because many purchases of goods can be easily postponed. In slack periods the demand for consumer durables and plant and equipment slumps while during booms much of the transitory increases in income is allocated to such spending. Thus the generally slow growth in GNP in the United States from 1973 to 1980 was reflected in disproportionately slow growth in the manufacturing sector.

The relation between the growth of manufacturing and the overall growth of the economy can be summarized statistically by regressing

7. An increase of 1 percent in productivity growth in (Hicks-neutral) U.S. manufacturing that was reflected in a reduction of 1 percent in the relative price of manufactured goods would only raise employment of labor and capital if the demand for manufactured goods was elastic. In fact, regressions relating the demand for manufactured goods to income and the relative price of such products suggest a price elasticity of about -0.7, so that more rapid (neutral) productivity growth would reduce rather than raise employment and capital formation devoted to manufacturing. The requirements for increased employment as a result of increased capital formation are even more stringent. In addition to the relative price effect of a productivity rise in manufacturing, aggregate real incomes would be higher by a quarter of a percent, and of that about a quarter, or 0.0625, would be spent in turn on manufactured goods.

8. Two measures of manufacturing output provide somewhat different growth rates: the industrial production index of the Federal Reserve Board consistently suggests more rapid increases than the deflated value of manufactured goods output in the U.S. national income and product accounts.

changes in industrial production, $\%IP$, on changes in GNP, $\%GNP$. The regression for 1960–73 (annual data) is

$$\%IP = -3.84 + 2.24\%GNP,$$
$$(-5.2) \quad (13.19)$$

where $\%IP$ is the annual percentage growth in industrial production in manufacturing, $\%GNP$ is the annual growth in real GNP, and the numbers in parentheses are t-statistics.[9]

The equation confirms that industrial performance is a magnification of that of the overall economy. If GNP grows at 1.7 percent a year in this equation, there will be no increase in manufacturing production. However, for each percentage point increase (decrease) of GNP growth above 1.7 percent, manufacturing output will rise (fall) by 2.24 percentage points. As indicated below, when this equation, based on data from 1960 to 1973, is used to forecast annual average growth rates of industrial production in manufacturing for 1973–82 given actual GNP, it does so with remarkable accuracy:

	Actual	Forecast	Error
1973–80	1.8	1.4	0.4
1979–82	-3.6	-3.8	0.2

Regressions of value added in manufacturing against other elements of GNP yield qualitatively similar results. Thus there is no puzzle in explaining aggregate manufacturing production: it is almost exactly what one should have expected given the performance of the total economy.

Factor Supplies

Although the overall level of manufacturing output has matched its historical relation with GNP, the relation between output and input growth has changed. As a result of the decline in productivity growth in manufacturing since 1973, given rates of output growth are now associated with somewhat higher rates of employment and capital growth. A regression analysis indicates that, taking manufacturing output as given,

9. The regression for 1951–81 (annual data) is $\%IP = -3.42 + 2.18\%GNP$.
$$(-4.8) \quad (12.6)$$

the growth of manufacturing employment has been about 1.36 percent a year higher than it would have been in the absence of the decline in manufacturing productivity. Thus employment has actually held up better than might have been anticipated from past relations. Probably the reason most often suggested for the decline in U.S. manufacturing productivity is the failure of U.S. business to invest in new plant and equipment. Yet although there has been a marked decline in the growth of the capital-labor ratio in the economy overall since 1973, the measured growth of the net capital stock in manufacturing has been remarkably rapid. Although the ratio of the net capital stock to full-time equivalent employees in manufacturing grew at about 1.9 percent a year from 1950 to 1973, it grew at 3.6 percent a year from 1974 to 1980.[10] And, while historically the ratio of the net capital stock in U.S. manufacturing to the net stock in the rest of the economy declined (from 0.30 in the 1950s to 0.262 in the 1960s to 0.222 in 1973), since 1973 capital stock in manufacturing has actually grown more rapidly than in the rest of the private economy.

The increased commitment of plant, equipment, and R&D expenditures makes the decline in productivity growth in U.S. manufacturing since 1973 particularly puzzling. One question is whether the capital stock is accurately measured. Mismeasurement could be the result of an increase in capital and R&D devoted to meeting regulatory requirements such as safety and pollution, which do not show up as output. If one subtracts Department of Commerce estimates of the net capital stock devoted to reducing air and water pollution from the net capital stock in manufacturing, the growth in manufacturing capital is lowered from 4.5 percent to 4.2 percent a year.[11] Mismeasurement might also be caused by the premature retirement of capital that has become economically obsolete in changed economic conditions.[12]

Nonetheless, as these data make clear, there has not been an erosion in the U.S. industrial base. The decline in output and employment *shares* has been the predictable result of slow growth, while, paradoxically, the

10. Based on data presented in Martin Neil Baily, "The Productivity Growth Slowdown by Industry," *Brookings Papers on Economic Activity, 2:1982*, pp. 423–54.
11. See Frederick G. Keppler and Gary L. Ruttledge, "Stock of Plant and Equipment for Air and Water Pollution Abatement in the United States, 1960–1981," *Survey of Current Business*, vol. 62 (November 1982), pp. 18–25.
12. See, for example, Martin Neil Baily, "Productivity and the Services of Capital and Labor," *Brookings Papers on Economic Activity, 1:1981*, pp. 1–50.

slow growth in productivity has required unpredictably large increases in employment, plant and equipment, and R&D.

U.S. Manufacturing in Global Perspective

A comparison of the performance of U.S. manufacturing with that of other major industrial countries should be useful for separating the problems that are shared by other countries and therefore reflect broader global forces from those unique to the United States. A comparison might also assist in gauging U.S. comparative strengths and weaknesses. Proponents of a radical change in U.S. industrial policies contrast the ad hoc and laissez-faire policies of the United States with the systematic and interventionist practices abroad. While conceding there are marked differences in the degree to which foreign practices have succeeded, they argue that the conscious policy of managing the decline of older industries and the rise of new industries has been superior to the U.S. approach marked by neglect. Similarly, in European economies the broad provision of social services, the extensive rights to jobs enjoyed by workers, and the restrictions of plant closures have all been held up as worthy of emulation.[13] Opponents of such policies argue that they will delay adjustment, for the government is most likely to be captured by forces seeking to preserve the status quo, and strictures on mobility are likely to retard adaptation.

It is particularly important that international comparisons be made on the basis of performance since 1973, for policies that enjoyed success in an environment of strong global growth and economic expansion may not be appropriate for the current era of stagnation.

The commodity boom of 1972–74 and the inflation that accompanied it ushered in a new era. All developed countries have been plagued by low rates of investment, slow growth, and inflation. The problems associated with high inflation and energy shocks have destroyed the confidence of investors. They have learned from their experiences in 1974 (and again in 1979) that, at any time, a political disruption in the Middle East or a sudden increase in domestic inflation could force their governments to adopt policies that bring on a recession, creating excess

---

13. See, for example, Robert Reich, *The Next American Frontier* (New York Times Books, 1983).

Table 2-2. *Real Growth of Output and Trade in Major Industrial Economies, 1960–80*

Average annual percentage change[a]

Country and period	Gross domestic product	Government consumption	Gross fixed capital formation	Private final consumption	Manufacturing production		
					Heavy manufacturing	Light manufacturing	Total manufacturing
Developed countries							
1960–73	5.0	3.7	6.3	4.8	6.7	4.5	6.2
1973–80	2.4	3.0	1.0	2.7	1.8	1.3	2.0
Developing countries							
1960–73	5.8	7.1	7.4	5.0	9.5	5.4	7.8
1973–80	5.4	7.6	10.2	4.6	5.6	3.5	5.9
United States[b]							
1960–73	4.1	2.8	4.5	4.2	5.9	4.4	5.4
1973–80	2.3	2.2	−0.4	2.7	1.6	2.0	1.8
Japan[c]							
1960–73	10.4	5.8	14.4	9.4	n.a.	n.a.	12.5
1973–80	3.8	4.2	1.8	3.2	n.a.	n.a.	2.9
Europe							
1960–73	4.8	4.1	5.6	4.8	6.0	4.4	5.7
1973–80	2.3	3.0	1.0	2.6	1.4	1.1	1.6

Sources: United Nations, *1981 Statistical Yearbook* (New York: UN, 1982); Organization for Economic Cooperation and Development, *National Accounts, 1951–1980*, vol. 1: *Main Aggregates* (Paris: OECD, 1982); and United Nations, *Yearbook of Industrial Statistics* (New York: UN, 1972, 1980).
n.a. Not available.
a. Compounded annually.
b. Available data for heavy and light manufacturing production include Canada.
c. Revision of Japanese data now under way in Japan may make the years before 1965 incomparable.

capacity for investors. As reported in table 2-2, after 1973 the rate of investment slumped in market economies; the growth of the heavy manufacturing industries was cut; and consumption expenditures rose as a share of GDP. Industries with long gestation periods for investment, such as steel and shipbuilding, have been particularly hard hit by the post-1973 slump. There is insufficient demand for the products of plants that were built on the basis of overoptimistic projections of market growth in the late 1960s.

Measured by a variety of indicators, the relative performance of U.S. manufacturing has improved since 1973. The declines in the growth of manufacturing production, productivity growth, employment, and investment in manufacturing were all smaller in the United States than in other industrial nations. In table 2-3, I report rates of growth for GNP and manufacturing production in the major industrial economies. Although the growth rate in the United States was among the slowest before 1973, since that time U.S. growth has been quite typical for a

Table 2-3. *Growth in Gross Domestic Product and Manufacturing Production in Major Industrial Economies, 1960–80*
Average annual percentage change[a]

	Gross domestic product[b]		Manufacturing production[c]	
Country	1960–73	1973–80	1960–73	1973–80
United States	4.1	2.3	5.4	1.8
France	5.6	2.8	5.0	1.3
Germany	4.5	2.3	5.1	1.1
Japan	10.4	3.8	12.5	2.9
OECD	5.0	2.5	6.0	1.7
United Kingdom	3.1	0.9	3.0	−2.2

Sources: OECD, *National Accounts, 1951–1980*, vol. 1: *Main Aggregates;* OECD, *Main Economic Indicators: Historical Statistics, 1960–1979* (Paris: OECD, 1980); and OECD, *Indicators of Industrial Activity, 1982-IV* (Paris: OECD, 1982).
  a. Compounded annually.
  b. GDP data based on 1975 prices.
  c. Manufacturing production index, 1975 = 100.

developed country.[14] From 1973 to 1980 the average annual increase of 2.3 percent in U.S. gross domestic product was about the same as that in other developed countries (an increase of 2.5 percent in the Organization for Economic Cooperation and Development), and U.S. manufacturing production grew at about the same average rate as that in the OECD as a whole (1.8 and 1.7, respectively). Although trailing behind the growth rate of Japan, manufacturing production grew more rapidly in the United States than in Germany, France, the United Kingdom, or the OECD.

It is in Europe rather than in the United States that employment is undergoing (absolute) deindustrialization. Compared with historical relationships to overall GNP, industrial production in Japan has been abnormally strong while in Europe production has been unusually weak. Regressions relating industrial production to GNP in European countries from 1960 to 1973 substantially overpredict the level of industrial production in 1980. For Japan, they underpredict industrial production (by 12 percent in 1980).

In table 2-4, I report growth rates in industrial output for several industries. U.S. output growth from 1973 to 1980 for food and related products, textiles, and chemicals was more rapid than that of either Germany or Japan. U.S. growth in apparel, glass, and fabricated metals

14. In fact, U.S. industrial production from 1973 to 1980 grew as rapidly as that in all major industrial economies.

Table 2-4. *Growth in Manufacturing Output, Selected Developed Countries, 1963–73 and 1973–80*
Average annual percentage change[a]

Category and period	ISIC number[b]	United States	Germany	Japan	OECD Europe	OECD total
Food, beverages, and tobacco	31					
1963–73		3.4	4.0	5.9	4.2	4.0
1973–80		3.0	1.8	1.3	2.2	2.3
Textile products	321					
1963–73		2.7	1.5	5.7	1.7	2.6
1973–80		1.0	−1.9	1.6	−1.1	−0.5
Chemical products	351, 352					
1963–73		7.9	9.0	13.7	8.8	8.9
1973–80		4.0	1.5	2.4	1.7	2.7
Basic metals	37					
1963–73		4.2	4.8	14.2	4.9	5.6
1973–80		−3.2	−0.8	1.0	−0.3	−0.9
Metal products	381					
1963–73		5.5	5.1	15.7	5.3	6.7
1973–80		0.6	1.0	2.1	0.1	0.5
Nonelectrical machinery	382					
1963–73		6.7	3.3	13.7	3.8	5.1
1973–80		3.3	1.5	5.0	1.9	2.7
Electrical machinery	383					
1963–73		6.5	8.5	18.1	6.8	7.9
1973–80		2.8	1.9	8.2	1.8	3.5
Transportation equipment	384					
1963–73		3.7	5.8	17.5	5.3	6.0
1973–80		1.1	1.4	4.7	1.1	1.2

Source: OECD, *Industrial Production* (Paris: OECD), various issues.
n.a. Not available.
a. Compounded annually.
b. International standard industrial classification code.

was also more rapid in those years (not shown in the table). Although U.S. growth lagged behind Japan in the various engineering categories for the same period, it trailed German growth only in metal products and transportation equipment.[15]

15. The latter year, 1980, was a recession year in the United States. Comparisons over the 1973–79 period show that the increase in U.S. growth of 24.2 percent in nonelectrical machinery was accomplished considerably faster than the rise of 18.7 percent recorded for the same industry in Japan.

Employment

The employment record of the U.S. manufacturing sector may come as an even greater surprise to those concerned about U.S. deindustrialization: from 1973 to 1980, although its growth rate was relatively sluggish, the United States increased its employment in manufacturing faster than any other major industrial country including Japan (see table 2-5). Moreover, since the length of the average workweek declined more rapidly abroad, the relatively larger growth in U.S. manufacturing employment is even more conspicuous. The comparison between U.S. and Japanese employment growth shown in table 2-6 indicates that in 1973–80 Japanese employment in sectors such as transportation, electrical machinery, iron and steel, nonelectrical machinery, chemical products, and nonferrous metal grew less rapidly or declined more than that in the United States.

As the case of Japan makes clear, in the current global environment of relatively slow growth in demand, rapid increases in productivity do not necessarily increase employment. Indeed, compared with the United States, the faster increases in Japanese productivity have entailed the more rapid process of labor-force deindustrialization. In the case of Europe, employment opportunities in manufacturing have decreased because faster productivity growth has been combined with relatively slower growth in output.

Capital Formation

In table 2-7, I contrast data for gross fixed investment in manufacturing in the United States and industrial European countries. The sluggish growth of such investment in Europe is apparent; only in France was it above its 1970 levels in 1979. When one compares the ratios of foreign investment in manufacturing with overall gross fixed investment in those countries, it can be seen that, in contrast to the United States, most foreign economies are allocating a smaller proportion of their new capital formation to industrial production than they did in 1970.

Just as an automobile may be decelerating and yet going faster than another, so one country may have a declining growth rate for investment with a capital stock growing at a relatively faster rate. Thus capital stock measures are required. I report such estimates gathered by the OECD in table 2-8. The estimates indicate that, in contrast to its previous

Table 2-5. *Changes in Employment and Hours in Manufacturing, Selected Developed Countries, 1960–80*
Average annual percentage change[a]

Measure and period	United States	Canada	France	Germany	Italy	Japan	United Kingdom	Eight European countries[b]	Eight European countries plus Canada and Japan
Employment									
1960–80	1.0	1.3	0.6	-0.4	1.2	1.6	-0.9	-0.1	0.4
1960–73	1.5	1.9	1.2	0.5	1.4	3.0	-0.5	0.5	1.1
1973–80	0.8	0.3	-1.2	-1.8	0.1	-0.8	-2.2	-1.5	-1.3
Aggregate hours									
1960–80	0.9	1.0	-0.1	-1.3	-0.3	0.8	-1.7	-1.1	-0.5
1960–73	1.6	1.7	0.6	-0.2	-0.1	2.1	-1.2	-0.4	0.4
1973–80	0.7	-0.3	-2.1	-2.6	-0.1	-0.7	-2.9	-2.3	-1.7
Average hours									
1960–80	0.0	-0.3	-0.7	-0.9	-1.5	-0.8	-0.8	-1.0	-0.8
1960–73	0.1	-0.2	-0.5	-0.8	-1.5	-0.9	-0.7	-0.9	-0.8
1973–80	-0.1	-0.5	-0.9	-0.9	-0.3	-0.1	-0.8	-0.8	-0.5

Source: Patricia Capdevielle and Donato Alvarez, "International Comparisons of Trends in Productivity and Labor Costs," *Monthly Labor Review,* vol. 104 (December 1981), p. 16.
a. Computed from the least-squares trend of the logarithms of the index numbers.
b. France, Germany, Italy, United Kingdom, Belgium, Denmark, Netherlands, and Sweden.

Table 2-6. *Employment in Selected Industries in the United States and in Japan, 1960–73 and 1973–80*
Average annual percentage change[a]

Category	ISIC number	1960–73 United States	1960–73 Japan	1973–80 United States	1973–80 Japan
Textile products	321	2.1	−1.1	−2.5	−4.7
Paper	341	0.9	0.7	0.0	−0.5
Printing	342	1.3	3.7	2.2	−0.1
Chemical products	351, 352	−0.7	−3.0	0.3	−1.9
Iron and steel	371	0.4	1.7	−2.0	−2.9
Nonferrous metals	372	n.a.	n.a.	−0.3	−2.0
Metal products	381	2.1	5.1	0.9	−1.6
Nonelectrical machinery	382	3.0	4.5	2.7	−1.4
Electrical machinery	383	2.2	5.2	1.2	−0.7
Transportation equipment	384	1.0	4.5	−0.9	−1.2
All manufacturing	3	1.2	2.6	0.3	−1.2

Source: *United Nations, Yearbook of Industrial Statistics* (New York: UN, 1967, 1977, 1980, 1981).
n.a. Not available.
a. Compounded annually.

performance, the capital stock in U.S. manufacturing grew more rapidly than in foreign economies and, between 1976 and 1980, even faster than in Japan.

Research and Development

Since 1972, U.S. spending on R&D in manufacturing has grown as rapidly as it has in other industrial countries, thereby reversing the relative decline in U.S. spending that occurred in the late 1960s and early 1970s. During that time government-funded R&D in the United States was cut back, while R&D spending in other major countries advanced rapidly. From 1972 to 1980 the growth in business-funded R&D in the United States was similar to the R&D growth patterns of France, Germany, and Japan; and although government-funded R&D in the United States has not grown at the Japanese pace, it has exceeded the rise in support provided by the governments of France, Germany, and the United Kingdom.[16]

16. See Rolf Piekarz, Eleanor Thomas, and Donna Jennings, "International Comparisons of Research and Development Expenditures," paper prepared for the conference on International Comparisons of Productivity and Causes of the Slowdown, Washington, D.C.: American Enterprise Institute, September 30 and October 1, 1982.

Table 2-7. *Growth of Total and Manufacturing Gross Fixed Investment in Selected OECD Countries, Selected Years, 1963–80*

Index 1973 = 100

Country and total or sector investment	1963	1970	1978	1979	1980
United States					
Total	59	77	109	112	108
Manufacturing	63	93	134	159	178
Canada					
Total	51	84	114	124	134
Manufacturing	52	101	98	106	124
France					
Total	51	83	109	112	118
Manufacturing	54	89	92	95	105
Germany					
Total	66	92	98	105	109
Manufacturing	71	121	93	101	109
Japan					
Total	31[a]	85	97	109	117
Manufacturing	32[a]	101	73	88	103
United Kingdom					
Total	63	92	98	99	98
Manufacturing	79	121	112	115	104

Sources: United States, Canada, France, Germany, and Japan are from OECD, *Flows and Stocks of Fixed Capital, 1955–1980* (Paris: OECD, 1983). United Kingdom is from OECD, *National Accounts, 1951–1980*, vol. 2: *Detailed Tables, 1960–1977* and *Detailed Tables, 1963–1980* (Paris: OECD, 1979 and July 1982, respectively).

a. Data are for 1964.

According to estimates of the Organization for Economic Cooperation and Development, which are based on a wide variety of indicators, the United States continues to dominate other industrial countries in its commitment to R&D. In 1977, for example, spending on R&D in U.S. manufacturing was equal to about 6.5 percent of the domestic U.S. industrial output. By contrast, spending on manufacturing R&D in Japan, the United Kingdom, and Germany amounted to 3.7, 5.0, and 4.0 percent of the industrial output, respectively. Indeed, privately funded R&D in the United States alone was equal to 4.4 percent of manufacturing product. In absolute terms and measured at purchasing-power parity levels, in 1979 the U.S. spent about 1.5 times as much as Japan, Germany, France, and the United Kingdom combined and employed about 1.3 times as many scientists and engineers. By contrast, in 1979 manufacturing employment in these countries was 1.5 times that in the United States. The OECD has also ranked industrial countries according to the

Table 2-8. *Growth Rates of Total and Manufacturing Gross Capital Stock, Selected OECD Countries, 1960–80*
Average annual percentage change[a]

Country and total or sector capital stock	1960–73	1973–76	1976–80
United States			
Total	3.6	3.0	3.5
Manufacturing	3.1	3.5	4.8
Canada			
Total	4.9	5.4	4.6
Manufacturing	4.8	4.7	3.3
France			
Total	5.2	5.1	4.4
Manufacturing	5.7	4.5	3.3
Germany			
Total	5.5	3.5	3.5
Manufacturing	6.5	2.3	2.0
Japan			
Total	11.9[b]	7.5	6.3
Manufacturing	12.8[b]	6.7	4.6

Source: OECD, *Flows and Stocks of Fixed Capital, 1955–1980.*
a. Compounded annually.
b. Data are for 1964–73.

percentage of manufacturing output spent on R&D in a variety of industry groups during the 1970s. In the OECD study the United States ranked first in manufacturing overall and in the electrical machinery, aerospace, general machinery, and transportation equipment categories.

As this brief comparison suggests, if U.S. performance since 1973 is considered to have been relatively poor, this should not be ascribed to a relative failure to commit resources either to capital formation or to R&D. Although U.S. manufacturers may have made inefficient use of U.S. capital stock and real R&D in manufacturing, the amount spent on these items by the United States has grown as rapidly as that spent abroad.

Productivity

Measured both in terms of the ratio of total output to all inputs and in output per worker-hour, U.S. productivity growth in manufacturing, as in the economy as a whole, has slowed in the period since 1973. Over the same period, however, there has been an even larger slowdown in

Table 2-9. *Growth of Labor Productivity and Output in Manufacturing, Selected Developed Countries, 1960–80*
Average annual percentage change[a]

Measure and period	United States	Canada	France	Germany	Italy	Japan	United Kingdom	Eight European countries[b]	Eight European countries plus Canada and Japan
Productivity[c]									
1960–80	2.7	3.8	5.6	5.4	5.9	9.4	3.6	5.4	5.9
1960–73	3.0	4.5	6.0	5.5	6.9	10.7	4.3	5.9	6.4
1973–80	1.7	2.2	4.9	4.8	3.6	6.8	1.9	4.2	4.7
Output									
1960–80	3.7	4.9	5.5	4.0	5.6	10.2	1.8	4.2	5.4
1960–73	4.7	6.3	6.6	5.3	6.8	13.0	3.0	5.4	6.8
1973–80	2.5	1.9	2.7	2.1	3.4	6.1	−1.1	1.8	2.9

Source: Capdevielle and Alvarez, "International Comparisons of Trends in Productivity and Labor Costs," p. 15.
a. Computed from the least-squares trend of the logarithms of the index numbers.
b. France, Germany, Italy, United Kingdom, Belgium, Denmark, Netherlands, and Sweden.
c. Output per hour.

productivity growth of other industrial nations, both in manufacturing and in their entire economies. Careful studies have been unable to provide convincing explanations for these slowdowns.[17] I will not attempt an investigation of them here. It should be noted, however, that despite some convergence in the period since 1973, the U.S. productivity growth *rate* in manufacturing remained the slowest of any major industrial country (see table 2-9).

Measured by output per worker-hour, however, the United States continues to be the world's most productive manufacturing nation. According to Roy, for example, in 1980 U.S. output per employed worker-year in manufacturing was about 16 percent higher than in Japan, 21.7 percent higher than in Germany, and 31.3 percent higher than in France.[18] However, the United States no longer leads in all industries. A 1981 white paper on international trade issued by the government of Japan indicates that Japanese productivity levels in 1979 were above those of the United States in steel (108 percent above U.S. levels), general machinery (11 percent higher), electrical machinery (19 percent), transportation equipment (24 percent), and precision machinery and equipment (34 percent).

Accomplishing Structural Change

The U.S. failure to promote industrial adjustment to structural change has been unfavorably contrasted with the explicit adjustment policies followed in Europe and Japan. It is therefore of some interest to compare the shifts in the U.S. industrial structure with those in other major economies to determine whether in fact U.S. industrial adaptation has been lagging. To explore this question I have used the data collected by the United Nations. These data provide fairly disaggregated information on industries at the three-digit ISIC (international standard industrial

---

17. See, for example, Assar Lindbeck, "The Recent Slowdown of Productivity Growth," *The Economic Journal*, vol. 93 (March 1983), pp. 13–34; and Edward F. Denison, *Accounting for Slower Economic Growth: The United States in the 1970s* (Brookings Institution, 1979).

18. Overall U.S. GDP per worker-year in the United States was 49 percent above that in Japan, 13.3 percent above that in Germany, and 7.7 percent above that in France. A. D. Roy, "Labor Productivity in 1980: An International Comparison," *National Institute Economic Review*, no. 101 (August 1982), p. 29. The Japanese Ministry of International Trade and Industry estimated the value-added labor productivity in Japanese manufacturing to be about 17 percent below that of the United States in 1980.

Table 2-10. *Changes in Employment Share in Manufacturing,*
High- and Low-Growth Industries in the United States, Germany,
and Japan, 1973 and 1979

Type of industry and year	United States	Germany	Japan
Selected high-growth industries[a]			
1973	30.4	39.7	31.0
1979	33.1	40.9	31.2
Percent changes in share[b]	8.9	3.0	0.6
Low-growth industries[c,d]			
1973	34.0	32.8	37.5
1979	32.0	29.8	35.1
Percent change in share	−5.9	−9.2	−6.4
Labor-intensive industries[c]			
1973	19.2	15.1	21.6
1979	17.3	13.1	20.4
Percent change in share	−9.9	−13.2	−5.5
Capital-intensive industries[d]			
1973	14.8	17.6	15.9
1979	14.7	16.7	14.7
Percent change in share	−0.7	−5.1	−7.5

Source: United Nations, *Yearbook of Industrial Statistics* (New York: UN, 1979, 1980).
a. Industrial chemicals, other chemical products, plastic products, machinery, electrical machinery, and professional goods.
b. Percent change in share is calculated as 100[(1973 share − 1979 share)/1973 share].
c. Textiles, apparel, leather, footwear, wood products, and furniture.
d. Iron and steel, nonferrous metals, metal products, and shipbuilding.

classification) level. First, I selected the group of industries that is generally considered to have high growth potential. This group is characterized by relative intensity in R&D and by rapid rates of technological innovation. The sample includes industries such as chemicals, plastic products, machinery, and professional instruments, which typically make up about 35 percent of manufacturing employment in major industrial nations. Next, I calculated the share of total manufacturing employment these industries accounted for in the United States, Germany, and Japan and compared growth in these shares for the 1973–79 period. (The results are shown in table 2-10.)

Although employment shares in all three countries increased, the rise of 8.9 percent in the U.S. share exceeded those of both Japan (with an increase of 0.6 percent) and Germany (an increase of 3.0 percent). A similar analysis was performed for a group of industries showing slow growth, both labor-intensive industries such as textiles, apparel, leather, footwear, and household furniture, and capital-intensive industries such as metals, metal products, and shipbuilding. This group also typically accounted for between 30 and 35 percent of total employment. In this case, Germany had the most rapid decline in the share of employment (a decrease of 9.2 percent), whereas Japan and the United States experienced shifts quite similar in magnitude. The United States moved out of labor-intensive industries faster than Japan, but the drop in the Japanese share of the capital-intensive group exceeded that of the United States.

These results should be treated with some caution because of the relatively aggregative nature of the industry divisions and the possible discrepancies in national classification schemes.[19] Nonetheless, they contradict assertions about the relative failure of the United States to shift resources toward high-growth industries and indicate that Americans have been about as successful as the Japanese in reducing the role of the low-growth industries.

Concluding Remarks

In this chapter I have pointed to the marked contrast in European economic performance before and after 1973, a contrast that is particularly evident in data on European industrial performance. European manufacturing production has increased by less than might have been expected, given the GNP of the respective countries. Employment has fallen and productivity growth slowed. Germany has been relatively successful in shifting out of industries exhibiting slow growth, but it has been less successful in moving into new ones. In fact, just as Americans have responded to the slowdown in manufacturing by decrying the shortsighted nature of their decisionmakers, in Europe the concern stems from excessive rigidity.

European governments have assumed much greater responsibility than the U.S. or Japanese governments for providing steady increases in standards of living. More job tenure is provided in Europe than is common in the United States. In the 1950s and 1960s these guarantees were costless, for rapid demand growth facilitated job retention and rising productivity growth made higher wages affordable. With the shocks and slow growth in the 1970s, however, governments were forced to make good on the guarantees. Partly because they were supported by

19. The shares in U.S. high-technology industry obtained in this exercise are similar to those of the more detailed analyses described below.

generous social payments and schemes such as indexation, growth in European real wages exceeded the pace warranted by changes in productivity and the terms of trade. This has squeezed profits, discouraged investment, and slowed growth.[20] With slow growth and high wages, firms wished to reduce their work forces. Governments were forced to support employment by establishing job subsidies, trade protection, and schemes for job-sharing, reductions in work hours, and early retirement; and extensive unemployment benefits had to be provided. Manufacturing employment declined, and the service sectors in Europe were unable to offer sufficient employment to new labor force entrants and those displaced from manufacturing.

Whereas European unemployment rates have been considerably lower than those in the United States for most of the postwar period, by 1982 the average unemployment rates in the United States and the European Community were 9.7 and 9.5 percent, respectively. Although these rates are similar, structural unemployment seems much higher in Europe. According to the OECD, in 1982 about 16.6 percent of the unemployed in the United States had been unemployed for more than six months. By contrast, in Germany, France, and the United Kingdom the long-term unemployed were 46.4, 66.5, and 54.5 percent of the unemployed, respectively.[21] In 1979 older males over age forty-five constituted 36 percent of all unemployed German males, whereas in the United States, older males were 17 percent of the unemployed. Similarly, older women were 29 percent of the unemployed in Germany and 15 percent of the unemployed in the United States.

There is, therefore, overwhelming evidence that the structural problems facing European economies far exceed those in the United States. As the Commission of the European Communities noted in a recent report:

It is in particular apparent that the Japanese and United States examples have in common a positive employment creation record, a more positive record of enterprise profitability, of labor cost adaptability to economic circumstances

---

20. See, for example, Jeffrey D. Sachs, "Wages, Profits, and Macroeconomic Adjustment: A Comparative Study," *Brookings Papers on Economic Activity*, 2:1979, pp. 269–319. According to Hill, based on data through 1976, profit rates of return in manufacturing in the United States and Japan show no evidence of a clear long-term decline. The data on European OECD countries for the same period consistently display downward trends. See T. P. Hill, *Profits and Rates of Return* (Paris: OECD, 1979), p. 118.

21. OECD, *Economic Outlook* (Paris: OECD, July 1983).

and—for reasons linked to social structure—of less onerous labor regulations that place constraints on the use of production capacity. By comparison, enterprise profitability has fallen to much lower levels over the past decade in Europe (especially in the United Kingdom and Belgium, but elsewhere too in lesser degree). The adaptability of labor costs to macroeconomic conditions and those of the enterprise is less in Europe.[22]

22. Commission of the European Communities, *European Economy: Annual Report 1982–83*, no. 14 (November 1982), p. 14.

CHAPTER THREE

Is Trade Deindustrializing America?

FREE international trade rests on the principle of comparative advantage. By engaging in trade, a nation can benefit from specializing in the production of goods in which it is relatively efficient and exchanging them for those in which other nations excel. Provided its cost levels are appropriately adjusted by exchange rate changes or monetary flows, the nation will be sufficiently competitive to pay for its import needs. Over time, comparative advantage may shift, however, and in principle an economy might lose its comparative advantage in an entire sector. Indeed, it is widely believed that the U.S. manufacturing sector is in the process of just such a decline—developed countries have become increasingly competitive with U.S. firms at the upper end of the technology spectrum while developing countries have penetrated the markets of those firms making more standardized products.

Framework for Analysis

Changes in international trade in manufactures are now widely viewed as a major reason for the declining share of manufacturing in U.S. employment. In this chapter, I show that this view is incorrectly applied to the 1970s, particularly the years between 1973 and 1980. I begin by estimating the role that manufacturing trade flows have played in aggregate U.S. manufacturing employment. First, I introduce a simple accounting framework and estimate the contribution of trade flows to manufacturing employment between 1970 and 1980. Next, I extend the analysis to 1980–82. The second part of the analysis accounts for the role of changes in relative U.S. price competitiveness and examines how such changes affect trade flows. I argue that both the positive record over the 1970s and the declines in 1980–82 were greatly influenced by the relative prices of U.S. manufactured products.

38

A separation of the effects on the economy of foreign trade and domestic forces begins with the identity $P = U + X - M$, where P is production; U, domestic use (consumption plus investment including inventories); X, exports; and M, imports.

Given data on total shipments, exports, and imports, any change in overall production can be decomposed into a change due to domestic use and a change due to the foreign balance. The use of raw data on trade flows and output will not, however, incorporate the *indirect* impact of trade. For example, when an airplane is exported from the United States, it embodies inputs from a wide variety of other industries, such as aluminum, tires, and computers. The ratio of total export shipments to total shipments in manufacturing thus understates the impact of exports. Similarly, when an import replaces a domestic product it entails a reduction in demand for the products of domestic manufacturing industries other than the industry competing directly with the import. In some cases, the induced effects even change the allocation of total value added between domestic and foreign sources. An increase in some chemical exports may require an increase in imported oil as a raw material, so that the net effect on the value of total domestic production is less than the value of the export. A complete accounting of the impact of trade should incorporate these indirect effects.

The indirect effects of trade in the United States were estimated for this study based on data for 1970, 1972, 1973, and 1980 on U.S. manufacturing output, exports, and imports. These data, available at the four-digit SIC code level, were converted into 1972 dollars and arranged to correspond with the industrial coding structure of the fifty-two manufacturing industries of the input-output table published by the U.S. Department of Commerce (see appendix table A-1).[1] Next, the input-output table was used to estimate direct and indirect output requirements. Thus for the output, exports, and imports of each manufacturing industry, I estimated value-added requirements for the originating industry and for all other industries. These estimates were used to derive the proportions of total value added in each industry that could be related to exports of all manufactured goods and to all manufactured goods assumed to be displaced as a result of manufactured goods imports;

1. The concordance provided by the U.S. Department of Commerce was used. See "Industry Classification of the 1972 Input-Output Tables," *Survey of Current Business,* vol. 59 (February 1979), p. 54; and U.S. Bureau of the Census, *1980 Annual Survey of Manufactures: Origin of Manufactured Exports,* M80 (AS)-6 (January 1982).

I then calculated a residual value-added related to domestic use. Employment effects were estimated under the assumption that productivity growth in the exports and domestic products of each industry was identical, so that employment proportions corresponded to those of value added.

Some caution is necessary in interpreting the results. First, it should be stressed that this is an exercise with ex post data rather than a simulation with a full-scale behavioral model. In relating growth to domestic use, exports, and imports, nothing is said about why these configurations should have occurred, and there is no accounting for the possible interactions between forces resulting in the behavior of these endogenous variables. For example, a fall in the price of imports may have forced domestic producers to lower their prices. Domestic consumption in the United States of both its own products and imports might have increased, but in the absence of import-price pressures, this consumption of domestic goods might have been lower. Second, because suitable trade deflators were not available, data on the current value of imports, exports, and output for each industry were deflated with industry deflators. This procedure required the assumption of similar price changes for exports of domestic goods and imports. The assumption appears weakest in the case of imports, but the methods followed here can also be employed under the alternative assumption that purchasers allocate a given dollar amount to the product of each four-digit industry (for instance, a unitary own-price demand elasticity) so that the deflated import measure indicates the quantity of domestic production that would replace a given nominal value of imports. Third, the input-output coefficients reflect the assumption of zero substitution possibilities between inputs. Fourth, changes in demand may have caused a notional loss of job opportunities, but need not have resulted in the actual displacement of workers, if there were fewer such opportunities than the number of jobs available as a result of retirements and voluntary quits. Finally, if imports had not been available, it is possible that domestic consumers might have purchased products from other industries rather than, as assumed here, the domestic industry that manufactures products similar to those imported.[2]

2. Note that any years chosen as the basis for comparison are likely to have some peculiar characteristics that could affect the conclusions of the study. Accordingly, wherever possible, comparisons are reported over a number of different periods. For a discussion of the methodological issues associated with exercises such as this see Walter

Table 3-1. *Value Added and Employment in U.S. Manufacturing Due to Foreign Trade and Domestic Use, Selected Years, 1970–80*[a]

Item	1970	1972	1973	1980
Value added (billions of 1972 dollars)				
Total	262.7	295.3	318.9	349.5
Foreign trade	0.6	−5.3	−3.3	2.6
Exports	22.4	24.0	30.1	52.9
Imports	−21.8	−29.3	−33.4	−50.4
Domestic use	262.1	300.7	322.2	347.0
Employment (millions)				
Total	19.34	19.10	20.11	20.24
Foreign trade	−0.05	−0.45	−0.34	−0.06
Exports	1.57	1.45	1.78	2.93
Imports	−1.62	−1.91	−2.12	−2.98
Domestic use	19.38	19.56	20.45	20.30
Addenda				
Percentage due to exports				
Value added	8.5	8.1	9.4	15.1
Employment	8.1	7.6	8.8	14.5
Percentage due to imports				
Value added	−8.3	−9.9	−10.5	−14.4
Employment	−8.4	−10.0	−10.5	−14.7

Sources: Based on data from U.S. Department of Commerce, Bureau of Economic Analysis, input-output tape; and U.S. Department of Labor, Bureau of Labor Statistics, employment and earnings tape.

a. Estimates of direct and indirect requirements based on the input-output table are used to calculate the proportion of value added related to manufactured exports and to manufactured goods displaced by imports. Value added related to domestic use is calculated as a residual, and employment allocated to foreign trade and domestic use is in proportion to value added in each two-digit input-output industry.

Value Added and Employment

In table 3-1, I report my estimates of value added and employment related to trade and domestic use in U.S. manufacturing for selected years from 1970 to 1980.[3] One first needs to compare 1980 with 1970.

S. Salant, *The Effects of Increases in Imports on Domestic Employment: A Clarification of Concepts*, Special Report 18 (Washington, D.C.: National Commission on Manpower Policy, 1978); and Charles S. Pearson, *Trade Employment and Adjustment* (Ottawa: Institute for Research on Public Policy, April 1981).

3. There have been a number of studies similar to this with somewhat different emphases. Krueger estimates, for example, that between 1970 and 1976 the average two-digit industry experienced an annual decline in job opportunities of about four-tenths of a percent resulting from increased imports. See Anne O. Krueger, "Protectionist Pressures, Imports, and Employment in the United States," National Bureau of Economic Research, Working Paper 461 (Cambridge, Mass.: NBER, March 1980), p. 20.

Baldwin decomposed employment by industry into an effect attributable to income

Because in both these years the capacity utilization levels in manufacturing were similar, the data are less contaminated by business-cycle effects.[4] In 1970 the value added related to manufacturing exports amounted to 8.5 percent of overall value added in manufacturing, while the production of manufactured imports at home would have raised value added in manufacturing by 8.3 percent. As shown in the table, by 1980 these shares had grown considerably—to 15.1 percent for exports and 14.4 percent for imports.[5] Thus during the 1970–80 period the increase in net value added due to the trade balance raised value added in manufacturing by 0.5 percent (in 1972 dollars).[6] Although net value added due to trade was $0.6 billion in 1970, it amounted to $2.6 billion in 1980 (both measured in 1972 dollars). Because products making up U.S. manufactured imports have lower output per worker when produced in the United States than products making up U.S. exports, net jobs relating to trade appear as negative values in each year in table 3-1. However, although there was a decline of 10,000 jobs due to trade between 1970 and 1980, the contributions of trade over the 1972–80 and 1973–80 periods were positive. Trade increased job opportunities in U.S. manufacturing by 390,000 from 1972 to 1980, and by 280,000 from 1973 to 1980. This can be compared with the corresponding total rise in manufacturing employment over these periods of 1.14 million and 0.13 million, respectively.

It is difficult to reconcile these findings with the widespread notions that foreign trade was having a major negative effect upon U.S. industrial employment in the 1970s. These perceptions can in part be explained by the inappropriate use of statistics and in part by the particular attention commanded by a few large industries such as steel and automobiles.

---

elasticities at home and abroad and a "competitiveness" effect attributable to changes in relative prices and the like. See Robert E. Baldwin and others, *U.S. Policies in Response to Growing International Trade Competitiveness, Final Phase I Report* (University of Wisconsin, Center for Research on U.S. Trade Competitiveness, 1982), appendix A.

4. According to the Federal Reserve Board, capacity utilization in U.S. manufacturing in 1970 and 1980 was 79.3 and 79.1 percent, respectively.

5. This is somewhat higher than the 13.7 percent estimate of direct and indirect export-related employment of the U.S. Bureau of the Census. See Bureau of the Census, *1980 Annual Survey of Manufactures.*

6. Note in table 3-1 that because products making up U.S. manufacturing imports are more labor-intensive (have lower output per worker) when produced in the United States than those making up U.S. exports, in 1973 net job opportunities relating to trade were negative even though net value added relating to trade was positive.

Generally those seeking to denigrate U.S. manufacturing prowess point to the declining U.S. share in global manufactured goods exports. And, indeed, from 1970 to 1980 the U.S. share of the *value* of manufactured exports from developed market economies declined from 17.4 percent to 15.4 percent. However, this measure is obviously inappropriate for the purposes of this study. For employment the data on U.S. manufactured trade *volumes* are more germane: the volume of U.S. manufactured exports increased by 101.5 percent from 1970 to 1980, whereas manufactured imports rose only 72.0 percent.[7]

Trade Flows and Relative Prices

As I show below, several real-dollar devaluations in the 1970s were important in determining these trade flows. There is some controversy about the empirical evidence linking trade flows to relative price changes. Those claiming to find no relation generally seek a contemporaneous response.[8] Statistical studies that look for lags over periods of at least three years find sizable effects.[9] Thus, claims to the contrary notwith-

7. United Nations, *Monthly Bulletin of Statistics*, vol. 36 (December 1982), pp. xxiv–xxv. By contrast, the increase in manufactured exports volumes in Japan, Germany, and all developed countries from 1970 to 1980 was 155.7, 71.0, and 90.3 percent, respectively.

8. In a prominent General Agreement on Tariffs and Trade (GATT) study, the authors argue that real exchange rates have not had the predicted effects on trade balances, concluding: "In general—only by invoking long lags, often of two years or more—between exchange rate change and the *initial* impact on the trade balance would it be possible to salvage even partially the conventional view." See Richard Blackhurst and Jan Tumlir, "Trade Relations under Flexible Exchange Rates," *GATT Studies in International Trade*, 8 (Geneva: GATT, 1980), p. 27.

9. See Michael C. Deppler and Duncan M. Ripley, "The World Trade Model: Merchandise Trade," International Monetary Fund, *Staff Papers*, vol. 25 (March 1978), pp. 147–206; Rudiger Dornbusch and Paul Krugman, "Flexible Exchange Rates in the Short Run," *Brookings Papers on Economic Activity, 3:1976*, pp. 537–76; Helen B. Junz and Rudolph R. Rhomberg, "Price Competitiveness in Export Trade among Industrial Countries," *American Economic Review*, vol. 63 (May 1973, *Papers and Proceedings, December 1972*), pp. 412–18; Stephen P. Magee, "Prices, Incomes, and Foreign Trade," in Peter B. Kenen, ed., *International Trade and Finance: Frontiers for Research* (Cambridge University Press, 1975), pp. 175–252; Mordechai E. Kreinen, "The Effect of Exchange Rate Changes on the Prices and Volume of Foreign Trade," International Monetary Fund, *Staff Papers*, vol. 24 (July 1977), pp. 297–329; Irving B. Kravis, Robert E. Lipsey, and Dennis M. Bushe, "Prices and Market Share in International Machinery Trade," National Bureau of Economic Research Working Paper 521 (Cambridge, Mass.: NBER, July 1980); and Ray C. Fair, "Estimated Effects of Relative Prices on Trade Shares," NBER Working Paper 696 (Cambridge, Mass.: NBER, June 1981).

standing, U.S. performance reflects the growing sensitivity of trade flows to changes in relative prices, manifested through changes in the exchange rate of the dollar. From 1970 to 1980 there was a marked improvement in U.S. relative price competitiveness that took the form of a real depreciation of the U.S. dollar. And the real increase in the manufacturing trade balance can be ascribed in part to the effects of the dollar devaluations in 1971, 1973, and 1978–79.[10]

Extending the Analysis to 1980–82

In my analysis above I showed that from 1973 through 1980 U.S. trade made positive contributions to employment in manufacturing. But since 1980 the influence of foreign trade upon U.S. manufacturing employment has changed dramatically.

A substantial proportion of the decline in U.S. manufacturing employment from 1980 to 1982 was due to changes in trade flows, particularly exports. Between these two years the volume of U.S. manufactured goods exports declined 17.4 percent. The volume of imports of manufactured goods rose 8.3 percent.[11] As estimated above, employment due to manufactured exports in 1980 was 2.93 million. Since output per employee in manufacturing was similar in 1980 and 1982, employment and output due to trade most likely declined proportionally. This suggests that an employment decline of 513,000 persons for 1980–82, or about 34 percent of the total 1.51 million decline in manufacturing employment, was due to the fall in manufactured exports.

The jobs lost because of increased imports can be estimated with either of two assumptions. As estimated above, imports displaced 2.98 million U.S. jobs in 1980. If one assumes that rising import volumes added proportionately to this job displacement, the 8.3 percent rise in import volumes between 1980 and 1982 displaced an additional 240,000 jobs in the United States. Alternatively, if U.S. demand is assumed to rise with domestic prices and U.S. production is reduced by an amount equal to the higher value of imports, the estimated job loss is negligible since import values and domestic prices both rose by about 14 percent.

I noted in chapter 2 that U.S. industrial production from 1980 to

10. Price sensitivity is a major source of the decline in the U.S. manufacturing trade balance from 1980 to 1982.

11. Import and export volumes are from the Foreign Trade Division of the Bureau of the Census.

1982 was quite precisely predicted given GNP. A regression calculated through 1980 forecasts a decline of industrial production of 6.8 percent. In fact, the decline was 6.2 percent. This finding creates a puzzle, for given the effects of manufactured goods trade, a larger decline in manufacturing production might have been expected. Apparently there were unusual offsetting sources of strength in domestic manufacturing. One of these was the production of defense and space equipment. From 1980 to 1982 production of this equipment increased by 11.4 percent and had a weight of about 7.5 percent in total value added in manufacturing.[12] Industrial production unrelated to either defense or exports declined by 6.0 percent, close to what should have been expected.

Manufactured Goods Trade

What lies behind the recent erosion of U.S. international competitiveness? No single measure can adequately capture the numerous factors that determine a country's success in international markets. Some of the factors that complicate the task of explaining performance are the heterogeneous nature of the goods entering international trade; differences in marketing, servicing, and reputation for quality; and the availability of trade financing and other forms of government support. These factors are unlikely to change radically in the short run in which fluctuations in the business cycle and in relative product prices are the major determinants of fluctuations in trade volumes. Accordingly, I estimate a set of simple econometric equations that explicitly model the major short-run determinants of trade flows and capture the long-run effects in trend variables.

The volume of U.S. exports is explained in these estimates by a set of variables that captures the growth in overall global economic activity plus the current and lagged values of the relative prices of U.S. manufactured goods exports (see table 3-2). Long-term global economic activity is proxied by a time trend. Short-term activity is represented by deviations from the trend of the volume of exports of the major industrial countries besides the United States, and the level of industrial production in the "rest of the world" (Europe, Japan, and Canada); the relative price variable is the ratio of the prices of U.S. manufactured goods to

12. *Economic Report of the President, February 1984*, p. 269.

Table 3-2. *Equations Representing the Volume of U.S. Exports
and Imports of Manufactured Goods, Selected Periods, 1964–83*[a]

	Dependent variable			
	Exports, QXM		Imports, QIM	
Item	First half 1964 to first half 1983	First half 1964 to second half 1980	First half 1964 to second half 1983	First half 1964 to second half 1980
Independent variable				
XROW	0.303	0.289	. . .	. . .
	(2.2)	(1.9)		
IPROW	0.569	0.575	. . .	. . .
	(2.4)	(2.2)		
ΣRPX	− 1.651	− 1.518	. . .	. . .
	(− 7.4)	(− 4.8)		
T	0.029	0.030	− 0.153	− 0.147
	(42.4)	(25.8)	(− 5.1)	(− 3.8)
GNP/GNP*	. . .	. . .	1.533	1.327
			(4.3)	(3.0)
GNP*	. . .	. . .	12.377	12.080
			(7.1)	(5.4)
ΣRPM	. . .	. . .	− 1.750	− 1.861
			(− 11.0)	(− 7.9)
DS	− 0.051	− 0.052	. . .	. . .
	(− 4.5)	(− 4.0)		
Constant	10.696	10.059	− 68.123	− 65.775
	(10.0)	(6.6)	(− 6.3)	(− 4.6)
Prediction error				
D8101	. . .	0.012	. . .	− 0.019
D8102	. . .	− 0.046	. . .	0.032
D8201	. . .	− 0.074	. . .	− 0.011
D8202	. . .	− 0.010	. . .	− 0.080
D8301	. . .	− 0.015	. . .	− 0.055
D8302	. . .	. . .	. . .	− 0.037
Summary statistic				
Standard error of estimation	0.035	0.036	0.041	0.043
Durbin-Watson	1.805	1.871	1.741	1.774

Sources: The dependent variables, *QXM* and *QIM*, quantity of U.S. exports and imports, respectively, are from the U.S. Bureau of the Census, Foreign Trade Division (Standard Industrial Classification SITC 5-8). The independent variables are as follows: *XROW*, total quantity of exports (SITC 5-8) from the rest of the world (developed market economies excluding the United States) from United Nations, *Monthly Bulletin of Statistics*, selected March issues; *IPROW*, manufacturing production in the "rest of the world" (OECD Europe, Canada, and Japan) from Organization for Economic Cooperation and Development, *Main Economic Indicators*, selected years; *RPX*, relative price of U.S. exports (the price of U.S. exports divided by the price of foreign competition) from International Monetary Fund, *International Financial Statistics* (data tape); Σ*RPX*, sum effect of *RPX* lagged over seven periods (the current and the six most recent periods); *T*, a trend variable (increasing by 1.0 in each time period); *GNP/GNP**, business cycle (a ratio of gross national product of the United States, 1972 dollars) from the U.S. Department of Commerce, Bureau of Economic Analysis; *GNP**, potential GNP of the United States (1972 dollars) from the Council of Economic Advisers; *RPM*, relative price of U.S. imports (unit-value index of imports divided by wholesale price index) from the Bureau of the Census, Foreign Trade Division, and the Bureau of Labor Statistics; Σ*RPM*, the sum effect of *RPM* lagged over seven periods; and *DS*, a seasonal dummy, set at zero for the first half and 1.0 for the second half of each year. Out-of-sample prediction errors for the dependent variable (true value minus predicted value) are denoted *D8101* for the first half of 1981, *D8102* for the second half of 1981, and so on.

a. Estimation of all equations is based on semiannual data. All variables except *T* and *DS* appear as logarithms, and *XROW* and *IPROW* appear as deviations from the logarithmic trends. Price coefficients are estimated as seven-period Almon lags using a two-degree polynomial. The numbers in parentheses are *t*-statistics.

the prices of manufactured exports of other major industrial nations, as computed by the International Monetary Fund.[13] All variables (besides the time trend) are entered logarithmically so that the coefficients can be interpreted as elasticities. The equations track U.S. export behavior from 1964 to 1983 quite precisely (with a standard error of 3.5 percent), and the coefficients are generally statistically significant with the appropriate signs. As shown in table 3-2, trade flows are responsive to both the activity and price variables. With no change in the relative price of U.S. exports, and trend rates of growth in world manufactured goods trade and rest-of-the-world industrial production, exports would increase by 5.8 percent a year (2.9 percent per half year). Over the long run (three and one-half years), each rise (fall) of 1.0 percent in U.S. export prices relative to export prices in the other major industrial countries lowers (raises) the volume of U.S. exports by 1.65 percent. After eighteen months only about half of the long-run effect will have occurred. The absolute values of the price coefficients are largest and most significant between six months to two and one-half years, but the effect continues to grow even after three years.

The import equations capture long-term shifts with a time trend and a measure of U.S. potential GNP. Short-term shifts are explained with a measure for the business cycle (the ratio of actual to potential GNP in the United States). The equations also include current and lagged values of the ratio of import unit values of manufactured goods to the prices of domestic manufactured goods. All variables in the equation are significant, and the specification fits the historical behavior of manufactured import values fairly well (with a standard error of 4.1 percent). The equations indicate that if the economy grows along a potential path of about 3.0 percent a year, with no change in relative import prices, manufactured imports will rise at about 6.5 percent a year. For each 1.0 percent deviation of GNP from this path, imports will deviate by about 1.5 percent in the same direction. The long-run price elasticity of 1.75 for imports is higher than that for exports. The mean lags are shorter. The most powerful effects come in the first eighteen months, but imports continue to be affected by price changes that occurred three years previously.

When the activity variables take on recent average values, these

13. An alternative specification using industrial production in other major industrial nations and a cyclical variable was also tested but provided poorer results.

equations imply annual growth of export and import volumes of 6.0 and 6.5 percent, respectively. Starting from a position of balanced trade, the manufactured goods trade balance will decline secularly, providing there is no fall in the relative prices of U.S. manufactured goods. However, an improvement of less than 0.25 percent per year in relative U.S. prices would suffice to ensure balanced trade in manufactured products.

During the 1970s U.S. relative export prices, as measured by the International Monetary Fund, declined by 13.5 percent. In the absence of this decline the equations for imports and exports from the first half of 1964 to the first half of 1983 in table 3-2 imply that U.S. export volumes in 1980 would have been about 22.3 percent lower than they actually were. Similarly, without the rise of 22.0 percent in the relative prices of imports, the dollar value of U.S. manufactured imports in 1980 would have been 25 percent higher. Thus the improvements in relative prices of U.S. manufactured products were an important part of the growth in U.S. employment due to trade, particularly from 1973 to 1980. But this adjustment had its costs: compared with trade in 1970, in 1980 any given volume of imported manufactured products required a 13 percent greater volume of manufactured exports to pay for it.

When the equations are estimated through 1980 and used to forecast trade volumes through 1983, they predict U.S. trade flows with reasonable accuracy, as shown in table 3-2. Thus it appears that trade flows have retained their previous historical relations to the variables in the equations, and that the underlying system has not undergone a substantial structural change in the period under consideration. As the table shows, in the first half of 1983 (the most recent period for which complete data are available) the equation for exports has an error of only 1.5 percent; on average, the out-of-sample predictions for exports are no larger than the within-sample standard error. With the exception of the second half of 1982 in which there was an unusually large decline in inventories at the trough of the recession, the import equation also tracks accurately. In the second half of 1983, a full three years out of sample, the import equation overestimates by less than 3.7 percent.

The equations for the full sample period, 1964–83, can also be used to indicate the relative contributions of the independent variables to more recent trade flows. Relative price effects have played the dominant role: from the first half of 1980 to the first half of 1983, the export equation indicates that the change in U.S. relative price competitiveness induced a fall of 32.8 percent in U.S. export volumes. Trend factors added about

17.5 percent to export volumes. But the global recession and decline in world trade depressed exports by 14.1 percent. The equations suggest that imports were increased by 16.7 percent because of the relative rise in U.S. prices and by 17.5 percent because of trend factors; imports were reduced by 6.8 percent because of the drop in the ratio of actual to potential GNP during the U.S. recession. The actual and forecast changes for trade flows in 1980–83 are shown below.[14]

| | Actual change | Forecast change due to | | | |
		Prices	Business cycle	Trend	Error
Exports	− 30.3	− 32.8	− 14.1	17.5	0.9
Imports	25.8	16.7	− 6.8	17.5	− 1.65

The equations also suggest a somber prognosis: only about three-fourths of the long-run effect of the erosion in U.S. price competitiveness from 1980 to 1983 had been felt by the second half of 1983. In the absence of an improvement in U.S. price competitiveness over its levels in the second half of 1983, the equations predict an additional drop of 21 percent in manufactured exports and a rise of 5.4 percent in imports in 1984 and 1985 due to 1980–83 changes in relative price factors.

Summary of Findings

The decline in U.S. exports from 1980 to 1983 was primarily the result of the erosion in U.S. price competitiveness; and despite its rise, U.S. import growth in 1983 remained depressed because of the U.S. recession. Economic recovery in the United States and a continuation of trends in 1983 relative prices could induce substantial further reductions in the U.S. trade balance.[15]

In one sense the results of this chapter, particularly those for the 1970s, confirm the judgment of those who believe that U.S. competitiveness suffered: a decline in the U.S. terms of trade for manufactured

14. Actual changes are from the first half of 1980 to the first and second halves of 1983 for exports and imports, respectively.
15. For similar conclusions see Robert A. Feldman, "Dollar Appreciation, Foreign Trade and the U.S. Economy," *Federal Reserve Bank of New York Quarterly Review*, vol. 7 (Summer 1982), pp. 1–9.

products was part of the adjustment process for maintaining U.S. external equilibrium. The exchange rate system was able to achieve this adjustment by channeling resources into U.S. manufacturing to help offset the erosion of competitiveness. And the magnitude of the price change required to bring about this adjustment was fairly modest.

The recent strength of the dollar reflects the change in the international role of the United States from a net lender to a net borrower, a change that has resulted primarily from the large government deficits. This strong dollar reflects the need to channel foreign goods into the United States to meet the rise in domestic consumption. In this sense, the growth in the manufactured goods trade deficit is a response to a change in economic structure. But it is not a change that has resulted from shifts in U.S. or foreign industrial policies or prowess; it is rather a change that reflects the budgetary decisions of the U.S. government.

From 1973 to 1980, partly because of the real devaluation of the dollar, foreign trade provided a net addition to output and jobs in U.S. manufacturing. From 1980 to 1982 the erosion in relative price competitiveness was the source of the declines in U.S. employment due to manufactured goods trade. Changes in the real exchange rate have been effective in moving the U.S. current account toward equilibrium, as determined by expenditure patterns. In 1970 and in 1980 the current account was a similar percentage of GNP. This stability was accomplished in part by growth in the manufactured goods trade balance because of the real devaluation of the dollar. In the 1980s the shift in the United States toward large full-employment government deficits unmatched by lower private consumption entails a current account deficit as the savings of foreigners helps finance the U.S. government borrowing. This is accomplished in part by a decline in the manufactured goods trade balance achieved through real appreciation. If these trade flows are viewed as undesirable, policies to lower full-employment government deficits should be considered.

The decline in the manufactured goods trade balance from 1980 to 1983 was not the result of a sudden erosion in U.S. international competitiveness brought about by foreign industrial and trade policies. It is predictable given previous trends and current levels of economic activity and relative prices. In the absence of a substantial decline in the dollar in 1984, price pressure will continue to cut off foreign markets for domestic producers in 1984 and 1985.

CHAPTER FOUR

Structural Change in Industry

THE NOTION of deindustrialization examined thus far has been that of manufacturing in the aggregate. But the concern about trade and other sources of structural change also relates to the effects on interindustry and interregional mobility. If the pace of structural change has accelerated, there could be a rise in the dislocation costs imposed on workers and communities even if, in the aggregate, the growth in employment is unaffected.[1]

It is important, however, that dislocation due to structural change be distinguished from dislocation due to slow economic growth. Given the overall slowdown in the growth rate of the U.S. economy from 1973 to 1982, more dislocation is expected. But has there been an increase in the structural change in U.S. manufacturing associated with any given growth rate?

To measure the degree of structural change in the economy over time, I used an index based upon changes in the employment shares of industries (and regions) in the economy. This index, I, is formed by summing the changes in the shares over the period of comparison. Specifically, I is half the sum of the absolute value of the differences between sector shares; that is,

$$I = \frac{0.5}{n} \sum^{i} |ai1 - ai2|,$$

where $ai1$ and $ai2$ are the percentage shares of sector i in time periods 1 and 2, respectively, and n is the number of years between observations. Absolute values are used to provide equal weight to growing and

---

1. For the view that an acceleration in the pace of structural change is the real problem associated with "U.S. deindustrialization" see Barry Bluestone, "Economic Turbulence: Capital Mobility vs. Absorptive Capacity in the U.S. Economy," paper prepared for the 1983 meetings of the American Association for the Advancement of Science held in Detroit, Michigan, May 29, 1983.

Table 4-1. *Structural Change in U.S. Employment,*
Selected Periods, 1950–80

Average annual change[a]

Period	Total employment[b]	Manufacturing employment[c]	Total regional employment[d]	Regional employment in manufacturing[e]
1950–60[f]	0.77	0.86	0.45	0.60
1960–70	0.54	0.58	0.33	0.49
1970–80	0.60	0.47	0.61	0.70
1973–79	0.67	0.50	0.55	0.64
1974–80	0.51	0.65	0.58	0.75

Sources: Employment data are from Data Resources Incorporated and from *Employment and Training Report of the President, 1982* (U.S. Government Printing Office, 1983), pp. 255–58.

a. Index, $I = \frac{0.5}{n} \sum^{i} | ai1 - ai2 |$, where $ai1$ and $ai2$ are the shares of sector i (region) in periods 1 and 2, respectively, and n is the number of years between observations.

b. Employment is measured in full-time equivalent employees in eleven one-digit sectors, based on sector categories from the input-output table from *Survey of Current Business*, vol. 59 (February 1979), p. 54: agriculture, forestry and fishery services; construction; durable manufacturing; finance, insurance and real estate; government enterprises; mining; nondurable manufacturing; retail trade; services; transportation; and wholesale trade.

c. Employment is measured in full-time equivalent employees in twenty-one two-digit manufacturing industries according to DRI grouping: apparel and products; chemicals and products; electric and electronic equipment; fabricated metal products; food and kindred products; furniture and fixtures; instruments; leather and products; lumber and products; machinery except electrical; miscellaneous manufacturing; motor vehicles and equipment; paper and products; petroleum and products; primary metal industries; printing and publishing; rubber and miscellaneous plastic products; stone, clay and glass; textile mill products; tobacco manufactures; and transportation equipment except motor vehicles.

d. Number of employees on nonagricultural payrolls in ten regions.

e. Number of employees on manufacturing payrolls in ten regions.

f. Regional employment data are for 1952–60.

shrinking sectors. The sum is multiplied by 0.5 so that if there is a total reversal of structure, the index will register 100 percent. If there is no change in structure, it will register zero.[2] Because measures of structural change are likely to be affected by the stage of the business cycle, it is important to use cyclically neutral measures for analyzing long-term trends. Data on U.S. manufacturing in 1960, 1970, and 1980 are particularly suitable for these comparisons because of the similar levels of capacity utilization in these years.[3]

When computed across the two-digit industries that make up the manufacturing sector, this index indicates that there were actually fewer shifts in the shares of industries in the 1970s than in either the 1950s or 1960s. (See table 4-1.) Structural change in employment in the U.S. economy as a whole increased slightly between the 1960s and the 1970s but remained below that of the 1950s. For both manufacturing and the

2. For the application of similar measures see United Nations, *Economic Survey of Europe* (New York, 1981).

3. The manufacturing capacity utilization index of the Federal Reserve Board registered 80.2 in 1960, 79.3 in 1970, and 79.1 in 1980.

economy as a whole, however, the indexes indicate increased regional shifts in the 1970s.[4]

An acceleration in the pace of change across U.S. regions could be caused by changes due to trade, technological change, or the pattern of demand; if regional dislocation accelerated because of these reasons, the indexes for structural change across both industries and regions would indicate increased change. The absence of increased change in industrial structure points to factors determining location decisions— such as regional wages, operating costs, taxes, regulatory policies—as the major source of increased regional shifts.

A second exercise confirms the stability in the shifts in manufacturing employment structure over the past two decades. A sample of fifty-seven industries from the three- and four-digit SIC codes was assembled. The industries chosen constituted about 85 percent of 1980 employment. For each decade, industries were split into quartiles on the basis of employment growth. While the average growth rate declined between the 1960s and 1970s, the dispersion across quartiles remained the same. In both the 1960s and 1970s the range between the first and fourth quartile was 50 percent. The decline in the mean growth of 11.6 percent from the 1960s to the 1970s was very close to the decline in each of the quartiles. U.S. industrial sectors grouped by growth rate in employment (percent) are shown below.

	Quartile			
	1	*2*	*3*	*4*
1960–70	44.0	22.0	10.0	− 5.6
1970–80	34.0	8.2	−2.8	− 15.4

Over the 1970s the third and fourth quartiles both had negative employment growth on average; over the 1960s there was negative growth in only the fourth quartile. Thus this analysis points to the impact of slow employment growth rather than to a speedup in shifts resulting from structural change as the primary source of the difficulties facing U.S. industry.[5]

---

4. For a more complete analysis of the impact of regional employment shifts see James L. Medoff, "U.S. Labor Markets: Imbalance, Wage Growth, and Productivity in the 1970s," *Brookings Papers on Economic Activity*, 1:1983, pp 87–128.

5. Of course I measure here only ex post structural change. In fact, if the economy has had more ex ante shocks, the lack of change might reflect increased rigidities.

The Role of Trade in Structural Change: Individual Industries

Although much of the discussion about U.S. deindustrialization has been about manufacturing as a whole, the discussion is heavily influenced by developments in just a few industries.

A Disaggregated Analysis

Tables 4-2 and 4-3 present disaggregated data on value added and employment to illustrate this. Some results in those tables may appear paradoxical. In particular, if employment due to trade in an industry is initially negative, indicating that imports, on balance, are displacing more jobs than exports are creating, then a labor-saving change in value added or productivity will expand employment due to trade by bringing it nearer to zero.[6]

The changes in employment reported in table 4-3 for 1970–80 for the manufacturing sector, divided into industries according to the input-output classification of the 1972 Census-SIC codes, reveal several facts. First, in the majority (thirty-one of the fifty-two) of the U.S. industries employment growth was positive; employment due to trade also grew in thirty-one industries. Second, generally the effects of trade on employment were smaller than those due to domestic use: in forty-two of the fifty-two industries the change due to trade was smaller in absolute magnitude than the change due to domestic use. Third, trade was not the reason for the drop in employment in most of the declining industries. In six of the nine industries in which employment fell more than 10 percent, employment due to trade actually increased; only in footwear and apparel was the loss due to trade greater than that due to domestic use. Similarly, employment due to trade increased in fourteen of the twenty-one industries in which overall employment fell: in only three industries—radio and television, motor vehicles, and miscellaneous manufacturing—was a decline due to trade larger than an increase due to domestic use.

6. Because of productivity changes, changes in value added in any sector may be in the reverse direction from the corresponding changes in employment. If value added per employee rises by x percent, value added must rise by x percent simply to keep employment unchanged.

From 1973 to 1980 the positive influence of trade was even more widespread—employment due to trade rose in thirty-eight of the fifty-two industries considered. However, overall employment declined in twenty-five of the industries, primarily because of domestic use. In none of the industries in which total employment declined was a positive effect due to domestic use offset by a negative effect due to trade. Although trade contributed to the employment loss in seven of the twenty-five industries, the decline due to trade was larger than the decline due to domestic use in only footwear and miscellaneous manufacturing.

Despite smaller changes due to trade than those due to domestic use, public perceptions may be exaggerating the role of trade because the effects of trade and domestic use have been positively correlated. For reasons unrelated to international trade, the U.S. manufacturing sector has been undergoing major structural shifts in output and employment because of changes in domestic demand and technology. The impact of trade has sometimes reinforced these domestic changes; in other cases, industries experiencing employment losses because of changes in domestic use have had only minor offsets as a result of trade. This correspondence between trade and domestic use is apparent at the relatively disaggregated level of the fifty-two input-output industries. From 1973 to 1980, for example, there was a 0.49 correlation between the contributions to value added from domestic use and those from foreign trade.

The Automobile and Steel Industries

Automobiles and steel have dominated the discussion about U.S. industrial performance and, indeed, since 1980 have accounted for a disproportionately large share of the loss in manufacturing employment. Allegedly, trade, and especially Japanese competition, have had a major negative impact on U.S. employment in these industries.

This section takes a closer look at the performance of the automobile and steel industries in the United States during the 1970s and then during the 1980–82 period. How much of the decline in employment in these industries was related to trade? In particular, how much was due to Japanese imports?

AUTOMOBILES. For the 1970s as a whole, an interval over which cyclical variations in demand were unimportant, the automobile industry is virtually the only industry whose experience fits the widely held view

Table 4-2. *Percentage Change in Value Added in U.S. Manufacturing Resulting from Foreign Trade and Domestic Use, by the Fifty-two Input-Output Categories, 1970–80 and 1973–80*[a]

Category	1970–80			1973–80		
	Total	Change due to foreign trade[b]	Change due to domestic use	Total	Change due to foreign trade[b]	Change due to domestic use
13. Ordnance and accessories	−20.7	3.0	−23.7	−15.7	3.0	−18.7
14. Food and kindred products	24.3	2.0	22.3	16.5	2.4	14.1
15. Tobacco manufactures	5.1	5.9	−0.7	−3.0	4.0	−6.9
16. Fabrics, yarn, and thread	13.3	−1.9	15.2	10.7	−0.8	11.6
17. Miscellaneous textiles	43.6	3.7	39.8	12.7	3.3	9.3
18. Apparel	24.7	−11.1	35.7	2.2	−5.9	8.2
19. Miscellaneous fabricated textiles	18.3	−1.9	20.2	3.5	−0.8	4.3
20. Lumber and wood products	28.8	0.6	28.2	12.0	4.4	7.6
21. Wood containers	−35.9	0.3	−36.3	−19.8	1.9	−21.6
22. Household furniture	26.5	0.6	25.9	−5.5	0.5	−5.9
23. Other furniture and fixtures	47.0	−7.5	54.6	17.0	−3.2	20.2
24. Paper products	33.1	0.5	32.6	11.5	2.2	9.3
25. Paperboard containers and boxes	17.3	1.0	16.3	0.5	1.6	−1.1
26. Printing and publishing	32.1	0.6	31.5	15.2	0.7	14.5
27. Chemicals and selected chemical products	30.5	6.8	23.8	6.7	4.8	1.9
28. Plastics and synthetics	108.0	18.3	89.7	16.1	9.0	7.1
29. Drugs, cleaning preparations	51.4	2.5	48.9	23.8	1.5	22.3
30. Paints and allied products	18.2	0.8	17.4	0.7	1.0	−0.4
31. Petroleum refining and related industries	30.0	−2.0	32.0	27.4	2.9	24.5
32. Rubber products	27.3	−0.6	27.9	−1.6	1.6	−3.2
33. Leather products	−19.0	−9.3	−9.7	−13.2	−6.3	−6.8
34. Footwear	−12.6	−21.6	9.1	−8.7	−15.9	7.3
35. Glass products	18.3	1.0	17.3	−5.0	2.6	−7.6
36. Stone and clay	14.0	−1.6	15.5	−6.7	0.3	−7.0

37. Iron and steel	-6.1	-3.4	-2.7	-22.5	0.5	23.0
38. Nonferrous metals	16.2	-0.4	16.6	-8.3	3.2	-11.5
39. Metal containers	-1.5	2.4	-3.9	-5.7	2.8	-8.6
40. Heating and plumbing products	19.5	2.2	17.3	-1.3	1.4	-2.7
41. Screw machine products	13.7	-4.4	18.1	-12.0	-1.5	-10.5
42. Other fabricated metal products	29.7	-1.5	31.2	7.6	1.5	6.1
43. Engines and turbines	27.2	19.1	8.1	1.4	10.0	-8.6
44. Farm and garden machinery	55.5	1.8	53.7	7.7	1.5	6.2
45. Construction and mining machinery	51.3	21.5	29.8	15.6	12.4	3.2
46. Materials handling machinery and equipment	20.2	3.9	16.3	4.8	3.3	1.6
47. Metal working machinery and equipment	26.7	-2.6	29.2	9.5	-1.6	11.1
48. Special machinery	-0.7	-1.6	0.9	-19.2	-0.2	-19.0
49. General industrial machinery	30.7	1.1	29.6	9.2	1.3	7.9
50. Miscellaneous machinery	49.2	9.0	40.1	30.8	8.5	22.3
51. Office, computing, and accounting machines	325.9	72.6	253.3	207.7	51.2	156.5
52. Service industry machines	40.1	8.0	32.1	-8.0	4.2	-12.2
53. Electrical and industrial equipment	38.2	10.6	27.6	10.8	7.8	3.0
54. Household appliances	28.9	2.3	26.6	2.6	3.0	-0.4
55. Lighting equipment	10.4	-0.9	11.3	-9.8	1.1	-10.8
56. Radio and television equipment	70.5	-12.5	83.0	51.8	-6.0	57.8
57. Electrical components and accessories	212.5	-6.2	218.6	109.7	-3.4	113.1
58. Miscellaneous electrical machinery, equipment, supplies	42.4	7.2	35.2	13.0	7.6	5.3
59. Motor vehicles and equipment	21.6	-15.4	37.0	-24.1	-5.5	-18.6
60. Aircraft and parts	11.1	16.9	-5.7	17.7	12.5	5.2
61. Other transportation equipment	21.4	-1.0	22.4	-14.3	1.1	-15.4
62. Scientific instruments	66.0	-0.6	66.6	32.8	0.4	32.4
63. Optical equipment	124.4	1.8	122.5	59.0	0.9	58.1
64. Miscellaneous manufacturing	19.7	-8.0	27.7	0.6	-5.7	6.3

Sources: Based on data from U.S. Department of Commerce, Bureau of Economic Analysis, input-output tape; Bureau of Industrial Economics, data tape for manufacturing output, exports, and imports; and U.S. Department of Labor, Bureau of Labor Statistics, employment and earnings tape. Figures are rounded.

a. See *Survey of Current Business*, vol. 59 (February 1979), p. 54, for definitions of the input-output categories according to the SIC codes.

b. Change includes both direct and indirect effects.

Table 4-3. *Percentage Change in Employment in U.S. Manufacturing Resulting from Foreign Trade and Domestic Use, by the Fifty-two Input-Output Categories, 1970–80 and 1973–80*[a]

Category	1970–80 Total	1970–80 Change due to foreign trade[b]	1970–80 Change due to domestic use	1973–80 Total	1973–80 Change due to foreign trade[b]	1973–80 Change due to domestic use
13. Ordnance and accessories	-5.2	4.0	-9.2	0.9	4.0	-3.2
14. Food and kindred products	-4.4	1.9	-6.3	-0.4	2.4	-2.8
15. Tobacco manufactures	-16.9	3.8	-20.7	-11.1	3.2	-14.3
16. Fabrics, yarn, and thread	-13.6	0.7	-14.3	-15.7	1.7	-17.4
17. Miscellaneous textiles	-8.6	5.5	-14.1	-14.5	4.3	-18.8
18. Apparel	-9.9	-6.3	-3.6	-13.7	-3.8	-10.0
19. Miscellaneous fabricated textiles	8.4	-1.6	10.0	-7.3	-0.4	-6.9
20. Lumber and wood products	15.2	1.1	14.1	-1.4	4.8	-6.2
21. Wood containers	-37.9	0.3	-38.3	-42.3	1.6	-43.9
22. Household furniture	0.9	0.5	0.4	-14.3	0.4	-14.8
23. Other furniture and fixtures	16.4	-4.5	20.9	6.0	-2.1	8.1
24. Paper products	1.5	1.5	0.1	1.6	2.5	-0.8
25. Paperboard containers and boxes	-8.9	1.0	-9.9	-8.7	1.6	-10.3
26. Printing and publishing	13.4	0.4	13.0	12.7	0.6	12.1
27. Chemicals and selected chemical products	6.2	4.4	1.9	14.0	5.5	8.4
28. Plastics and synthetics	-11.9	5.4	-17.3	-15.3	5.6	-20.9
29. Drugs, cleaning preparations	22.1	1.5	20.6	17.3	1.3	16.0
30. Paints and allied products	-6.9	0.4	-7.3	-5.9	0.9	-6.9
31. Petroleum refining and related industries	3.5	-0.6	4.1	2.6	4.2	-1.6
32. Rubber products	25.3	-0.5	25.8	5.0	1.5	3.5
33. Leather products	-27.8	-6.3	-21.6	-15.4	-5.5	-9.9
34. Footwear	-27.0	-15.9	-11.2	-18.2	-12.1	-6.1
35. Glass products	-1.4	1.1	-2.5	-8.4	2.6	-11.0
36. Stone and clay	4.6	-1.3	6.0	7.1	0.3	7.4

37. Iron and steel	14.2	2.5	11.2	13.0		13.0
38. Nonferrous metals	3.0	0.1	2.8	0.0	2.9	−2.9
39. Metal containers	−17.2	2.2	−19.4	−13.5	2.7	−16.2
40. Heating and plumbing products	16.0	2.1	14.0	5.0	1.6	3.3
41. Screw machine products	−8.7	−3.7	−5.0	−10.8	−1.5	−9.3
42. Other fabricated metal products	10.3	−1.1	11.4	2.3	1.7	0.6
43. Engines and turbines	21.8	17.8	4.0	11.2	12.3	−1.1
44. Farm and garden machinery	13.5	1.3	12.2	10.1	1.6	8.5
45. Construction and mining machinery	46.2	19.9	26.2	25.5	15.4	10.1
46. Materials handling machinery and equipment	30.8	4.7	26.1	8.4	3.5	4.8
47. Metal working machinery and equipment	17.2	−2.8	19.9	16.4	−1.5	17.9
48. Special machinery	5.3	−1.5	6.8	6.9	0.0	6.9
49. General industrial machinery	13.4	−0.7	14.1	11.0	1.5	9.5
50. Miscellaneous machinery	37.3	8.0	29.2	33.7	8.7	25.0
51. Office, computing, and accounting machines	50.1	16.1	34.0	52.1	19.3	32.8
52. Service industry machines	17.0	5.7	11.2	−4.9	4.5	−9.4
53. Electrical and industrial equipment	10.2	7.1	3.2	5.6	7.1	−1.6
54. Household appliances	−11.2	2.1	−13.3	−17.5	3.0	−20.5
55. Lighting equipment	6.3	−0.8	7.1	−6.0	1.0	−7.1
56. Radio and television equipment	−0.9	−5.7	4.8	4.8	−1.6	6.3
57. Electrical components and accessories	51.0	−7.8	58.7	34.8	−4.1	38.9
58. Miscellaneous electrical machinery, equipment, supplies	28.0	6.6	21.5	7.1	7.4	−0.2
59. Motor vehicles and equipment	−1.3	−11.1	9.9	−19.2	−6.4	−12.8
60. Aircraft and parts	−1.8	12.8	−14.6	24.3	14.6	9.7
61. Other transportation equipment	3.9	−0.2	4.1	−9.0	0.8	−9.8
62. Scientific instruments	34.9	−1.6	36.4	29.5	0.3	29.2
63. Optical equipment	24.0	0.3	23.7	13.7	0.2	13.5
64. Miscellaneous manufacturing	−1.8	−5.0	3.2	−8.0	−4.5	−3.5

Sources: Same as table 4-2.
a-b. See notes to table 4-2.

Table 4-4. *Employment in the Automobile Industry in Relation to Foreign Trade and Domestic Use, 1980 and 1980–82*
Thousands of jobs

Source of employment	1980	1980–82 change	1980–82 change as a percentage of 1980 employment
Foreign trade	− 146.3	− 8.4	− 1.1
Exports	110.2	− 25.4	− 3.2
Imports	− 256.5	17.0	2.2
Domestic use	935.1	− 75.6	− 9.6
Total	788.8	− 84.0	− 10.6

Source: Total employment is from Department of Labor, Bureau of Labor Statistics, employment and earnings tape. Employment related to trade is from the input-output analysis; and trade volumes in the automobile industry are from the Foreign Trade Division of the U.S. Bureau of the Census.

that the employment decline was due to trade and that without trade, employment would have grown. Yet even in automobiles, problems stem from domestic sources. As reported in table 4-2, of the 24.1 percent decline in the output of the U.S. automobile industry from 1973 to 1980 (category 59), 18.6 percent could be attributed to a decline in domestic use and 5.5 percent to changes in the net trade balance. Even if Japanese imports had remained constant during this period, the problems faced by the automobile industry and its suppliers would have been severe. A relative rise in wages in the automobile industry and the impact of regulation have raised relative prices of U.S. automobiles. Moreover, the increase of gasoline prices, fears of gasoline shortages, and after 1979 high real interest rates and depressed cyclical conditions have further suppressed the domestic demand for cars. Indeed, from 1980 to 1982 the dominant source of the decline in U.S. automobile employment was domestic automobile demand rather than foreign trade. As indicated in table 4-4, automobile employment related to domestic use fell by 9.6 percent compared to the 1.1 percent decline due to foreign trade during this period.[8]

8. From 1980 to 1982 the volume of imports of automobile vehicles, parts, and engines decreased by 2.9 percent. However, output per employee in the automobile industry increased over this period by 4 percent, so that imports translated into fewer domestic job equivalents (about 2.2 percent of 1980 employment). Contrary to popular perceptions then, imports had a positive effect on employment. Conversely, because of this productivity increase, the 20 percent fall in the volume of exports accounted for a 3.2 percent decline in jobs. Overall, however, trade contributed only 10 percent to the decrease of 84,000 jobs in automobile employment. The year 1978 was the cyclical peak for automobile production. An analysis of the 1978–82 period indicates that trade accounted for 9.4 percent of the 300,100 decline in automobile employment.

Constant share analysis further illustrates the limited impact of trade on automotive production. Even if the *share* of imports in automobile sales had remained at its 1978 level of 17.7 percent rather than increase to 27.8 percent in 1982, the decline in U.S. production would have been offset by only 22.8 percent. Japanese imports exerted little influence on automobile employment from 1980 to 1982. The value of Japanese motor vehicles and parts (CIF) shipped to the United States was $11.61 billion in 1980 and $12.9 billion in 1982.[9] From 1980 to 1982 the price rise of U.S. automobiles was 20.4 percent;[10] therefore, in terms of U.S. automobile equivalents, exports of Japanese automobiles to the United States actually declined by 7.7 percent. Furthermore, even if the Japanese share of retail sales had remained at its 1980 level of 21.2 percent rather than increase to 22.6 percent, the decline in domestic production would have been offset by only 13.3 percent.[11]

STEEL. During the 1970s the role of domestic use in reducing demand was greater in the steel industry than in automobiles. Reduced domestic use of iron and steel lowered output from 1970 to 1980 by 2.7 percent; from 1973 to 1980, by 23.0 percent. Even if foreign trade had not reduced domestic steel output by a total of 3.4 percent between 1970 to 1980, these would have been difficult times for the U.S. steel industry. From 1973 to 1980 net foreign trade partially offset (by 0.5 percent) the decline in U.S. output due to domestic use.[12]

More recently the impact of foreign trade on employment in the U.S. steel industry has been qualitatively different from the effect on automobiles, primarily because of the role of steel as an intermediate input. As table 4-5 implies, in 1980 only 6 percent of total steel employment was related to steel exports; however, an additional 17.3 percent was attributable to U.S. manufactured exports of other products. Similarly,

9. *Economic Report of the President, February 1984*, p. 289.
10. U.S. Department of Commerce, Bureau of the Census, *Highlights of U.S. Export and Import Trade*, FT990 (December 1980, December 1982).
11. The examination of the 1980–82 period omits the acceleration of Japanese sales between 1978 and 1982. If the Japanese share of retail sales had remained at the 12.0 percent level held in 1978, the decline in U.S. domestic production from 1978 to 1982 would have been offset by 23.7 percent. Sales and share data are from Motor Vehicle Manufacturers Association of the United States, Inc., *MVMA Motor Vehicle Facts and Figures '83* (Detroit: MVMA, 1983).
12. My measures of the effect due to trade include the indirect effects of trade in other products besides steel. Thus an important source of the output gains from trade in steel was the rise in U.S. exports of machinery.

Table 4-5. *Employment in the Steel Industry in Relation to Foreign Trade and Domestic Use, 1980 and 1980–82*[a]

Thousands of jobs

Source of employment	1980	1980–82 change	1980–82 change as a percentage of 1980 employment
Foreign trade	−61.4	−36.4	−9.1
Exports			
Steel	24.1	−13.4	−3.4
Other products[b]	68.8	−12.5	−3.1
Imports			
Steel	−91.2	−5.9	−1.5
Other products[c]	−63.1	−4.6	−1.2
Domestic use	460.2	−73.0	−18.3
Total	398.8	−109.4	−27.4

Sources: Total employment, exports, and imports of steel are from the American Iron and Steel Institute; trade volumes in manufacturing are from the Foreign Trade Division of the Bureau of the Census. Employment related to trade is from the input-output analysis.

a. The steel industry here refers to the industry called steel mill products by the American Iron and Steel Institute. This industry corresponds closely with SIC 3312.

b. Other manufactured exports.

c. Other manufactured imports.

the proportions of steel employment directly related to steel imports and indirectly to imports of other manufactured products were 22.9 percent and 15.8 percent, respectively. Thus steel employment is particularly sensitive to changes in U.S. manufacturing trade performance. This sensitivity is clear in steel employment behavior between 1980 and 1982. As shown in table 4-5, changes in steel trade from 1980 to 1982 led to a decrease of 19,300 jobs in the steel industry. The *total* trade-related effect on the steel industry between 1980 and 1982 was about 33.3 percent of the 109,400 jobs lost in steel.

Japanese imports had a minimal influence on steel employment. In 1980 the United States imported about 6 million net tons of steel from Japan, and in 1982, a little over 5 million tons; the shares increased from 6.3 percent to 6.8 percent. Had the Japanese retained their 1980 share of the U.S. steel market, and domestic products been purchased instead of Japanese products, the decline in steel output would have been offset by only 1.7 percent.[13]

13. If the Japanese share of imports remained at its peak level of 5.5 percent in 1979, the decline in U.S. steel output would have been offset by only 2.5 percent. Japanese import shares and volumes are from *Annual Statistical Report: American Iron and Steel Institute, 1982* (Washington, D.C.: AISI, 1983).

Two main points should be made about this analysis. First, it should be stressed that the methodology in this section assumes that, in the absence of imports, U.S. consumers would have purchased similar values of domestic products. However, this assumption is particularly unrealistic and overstates the employment possibilities of import reduction in automobiles and steel for a number of reasons. The surge in U.S. automobile imports was related to a relative rise in the demand for small cars that U.S. manufacturers were unable to meet. Similarly, the growth in U.S. steel imports from 1980 to 1982 was entirely in tubes, pipes, and fittings; the domestic steel industry was operating at close to capacity in its production of these items, which are particularly important inputs in the oil industry. Even if this analysis exaggerates the impact of trade, the point remains clear that domestic use has had a dominant influence on employment.

Second, as I have shown, contrary to popular perceptions Japanese exports of automobiles and steel did not contribute significantly to the declines in U.S. employment in these industries from 1980 to 1982. However, it should be noted that Japan exercised restraint in limiting its exports to the United States. Japanese steel imports remained fairly steady at about 6 million net tons from 1978 to 1982.[14] Japanese automobile export volumes were 1.4 million in 1978 and 1.8 million in 1982.[15] Thus the behavior of Japanese imports over the last several years does not fully reflect "potential" Japanese competitiveness.

Achieving Structural Change

In the trade literature it is customary to separate goods into three groups: goods that require the relatively intensive use of natural resources (Ricardo goods), goods that require high proportions of R&D or employ scientists and engineers fairly intensively (product-cycle or high-technology goods), and goods that use relatively standardized production technologies (Hecksher-Ohlin goods). In this book for the production characteristics categories I adopt the Ricardo (resource-intensive) and the product-cycle (high-technology) groupings and divide the latter Hecksher-Ohlin group according to relative capital-labor ratios into

14. From *Annual Statistical Report: American Iron and Steel Institute* (Washington, D.C.: AISI, 1983).

15. From Motor Vehicle Manufacturers Association of the United States, Inc., *MVMA Motor Vehicle Facts and Figures '83*.

Table 4-6. *Shares of Value Added and Employment in U.S. Manufacturing, by Production Characteristics of Industries, Selected Years, 1960–80*

Percent

Item and characteristic of industry	1960	1970	1972	1973	1980
Value added[a]					
High-technology	27	31	31	32	38
Capital-intensive	32	30	31	32	27
Labor-intensive	13	13	14	13	12
Resource-intensive	28	25	24	23	23
Employment[b]					
High-technology	27	30	28	29	33
Capital-intensive	29	30	30	30	28
Labor-intensive	21	20	21	21	19
Resource-intensive	23	21	21	20	20

Sources: Based on data from Department of Commerce, Bureau of Economic Analysis, input-output tape; Bureau of Industrial Economics, data base for manufacturing output, exports, and imports; and Department of Labor, Bureau of Labor Statistics, employment and earnings tape.

a. Computed for each input-output industry by multiplying gross output in 1972 dollars by the ratio of value added to output in the 1972 input-output table.

b. Derived from the Bureau of Labor Statistics series on employment and earnings. The series have been aggregated to the two-digit input-output industry and then to the production characteristics categories.

capital- and labor-intensive categories.[16] A second classification scheme I draw upon is the five major end-use categories—equipment, consumer durables, automobiles, and intermediate products. I follow the classification method used in the end-use categories of the Federal Reserve's industrial production index (adjusted to conform to the input-output categories).

Development of High Technology

The data in table 4-6 highlight the changes in the composition of U.S. output and employment in U.S. manufacturing. They indicate the long-run shift toward high-technology industries. The change in employment proceeded at about the same pace between 1970 and 1980 as during the previous decade, although the shift measured by value added accelerated

16. The ratio of employment to gross capital stock in 1976 at the three-digit SIC level was used to divide the Hecksher-Ohlin group. The detailed classification scheme used by Stern and Maskus has been matched with the fifty-two input-output categories as indicated in table A-1 of the appendix. See Robert M. Stern and Keith E. Maskus, "Determinants of the Structure of U.S. Foreign Trade, 1958–76," *Journal of International Economics*, vol. 11 (May 1981), pp. 207–24.

Table 4-7. *Growth of Fixed Capital, Hours Worked,*
and the Capital-Labor Ratio in U.S. Manufacturing, High-
and Low-Technology Industries, Selected Periods, 1950–80
Average annual percentage change[a]

Item	1950–60	1960–70	1970–80	1973–80
Fixed capital				
High-technology[b]	4.6	4.4	4.4	5.1
Low-technology[c]	2.8	2.8	3.0	3.3
Hours worked				
High-technology	2.8	2.7	1.7	1.6
Low-technology	0.2	1.0	0.0	−0.9
Capital-labor ratio				
High-technology	1.8	1.7	2.6	3.4
Low-technology	2.6	1.9	3.1	4.2

Sources: Department of Commerce, Bureau of Economic Analysis; see also Martin Neil Baily, "The Productivity Growth Slowdown by Industry," *Brookings Papers on Economic Activity, 2:1982*, pp. 423–59.
a. Compounded annually.
b. High technology: chemicals; machinery except electrical; electrical machinery; instruments.
c. Low technology: total manufacturing minus high technology.

somewhat. But from 1973 to 1980 the movement toward high technology accelerated by both measures. In the thirteen years from 1960 to 1973 the share of high-technology products in total value added increased from 27 to 32 percent. In the next seven years it rose from 32 to 38 percent. The acceleration in employment share in high-technology industries is even more dramatic; after increasing from 27 percent in 1960 to 29 percent in 1973, it rose to 33 percent by 1980.

Table 4-7 reports growth in capital stock, separated at the two-digit SIC level into high- and low-technology industries. Capital formation, like output and employment growth, has been more rapid in the high-technology industries. When one compares 1973-80 with the 1950s and 1960s, fixed capital and the capital-labor ratio show accelerated growth rates in both types of industry. Thus the slower output growth and productivity performance of neither sector can be ascribed to a failure to maintain investment.

Table 4-8 breaks down the striking divergence of high-technology industries from the rest of manufacturing into the parts accounted for by domestic use and foreign trade. Between 1973 and 1980 the output of high-technology products increased by 30.6 percent and employment rose by 15.7 percent; in industries characterized by other production processes, output grew sluggishly and employment declined. The compositional changes were related to growth resulting from *both* trade and domestic use. Although most employment growth in the high-technology

Table 4-8. *Changes in Value Added and Employment in U.S. Manufacturing Due to Domestic Use and Foreign Trade, by Production Characteristics of Industries, 1970–80 and 1973–80*[a]

Item and characteristic of industry	1970–80		1973–80	
	Domestic use	Foreign trade	Domestic use	Foreign trade
Value added				
High-technology	54.7	7.2	25.2	5.4
Capital-intensive	22.2	−3.8	−6.7	−0.6
Labor-intensive	20.7	−4.1	−0.2	−1.9
Resource-intensive	22.6	0.8	8.2	2.5
Employment				
High-technology	12.9	3.5	11.1	4.6
Capital-intensive	2.3	−1.9	−5.9	−0.1
Labor-intensive	1.8	−3.6	−6.3	−2.0
Resource-intensive	−0.6	1.1	−4.1	2.6

Sources: Same as table 4-6.
a. Same as table 4-6.

industries can be ascribed to the rise in domestic use, growth in employment from foreign trade was greater in high-technology industries than in any industry category. Foreign trade also raised employment in resource-intensive industries where domestic demand was sluggish. Stagnant or falling domestic demand, combined with a reinforcing decline in net foreign demand, thwarted growth in both capital- and labor-intensive industries.

End Use

Overall none of the major end-use or production characteristics categories grew more rapidly in the 1970s than in the 1960s. Among the end-use categories, however, growth of domestic use was most rapid in equipment from 1970 to 1980. Given the fairly widespread perceptions that the United States has been saving and investing too little and buying consumer goods on credit at excessive rates, the pattern of real domestic use is somewhat surprising. According to regressions similar to those above for U.S. industrial production, given the growth of GNP, U.S. expenditure on consumption goods (particularly consumer durables) has been weaker than expected. On the other hand, expenditure on machinery and equipment has exceeded previous historical norms. As a result, for real domestic use of U.S. manufactured goods, the share devoted to machinery and equipment rose from 20.6 percent in 1970 to 22.5 percent in 1980, whereas the shares devoted to automobiles, materials, and consumer goods each declined by approximately 1 percent.

Patterns of Domestic Use: Technology and Demand

Looking at the detailed data on industries and the product-cycle aggregation, one is struck by the degree to which most of the story of structural change can be told simply by looking at the data on domestic use. The change in output due to domestic use was weakest in the old U.S. industries such as tobacco, wood containers, leather goods, iron and steel, and metal containers. The highest increases in domestic use were all seen in high-technology industries. From 1970 to 1980, for example, output in office, computing, and accounting machines increased 253 percent; electronic components, 219 percent; optical equipment, 123 percent; and plastics, 90 percent. Of the high-technology industries, domestic use had a negative effect on aircraft only. Thus the patterns associated with the performance of U.S. industrial growth in the 1970s are all present in the data on domestic use: considerably more rapid output gains in high-technology and equipment industries; a decline in growth rates in all major production characteristics categories and end-use categories between the 1960s and the 1970s; particularly sluggish performance in U.S. labor- and capital-intensive industries; and weak growth of industries such as leather, wood containers, tobacco products, and metal products. Almost all these developments have been reinforced by the influence of foreign competition, although their directions and general magnitudes would be the same without the effects due to foreign trade.

Explanations of the accelerated shift toward high-technology production since 1972 often cite the influence of foreign trade or a speedup in the pace of technological change. But neither of these explanations seems sufficient. As shown in table 4-8, the accelerated shift is present even when the effects of trade are excluded. Thus trade is certainly not all of the story. As for faster technological change, table 4-9 shows that employment, output, and productivity (output per employee) in high-technology industries grew more slowly from 1973 to 1980 than they did in the 1960s. In fact, as measured by the growth in output per employee, the slowdown in productivity growth in the high-technology industries

Table 4-9. *Changes in Employment, Value Added, and Productivity
in U.S. Manufacturing, High- and Low-Technology Goods,
Selected Periods, 1960–82*
Average annual percentage change[a]

Item and type of technology	1960–70	1970–80	1973–80	1980–82
Employment				
High-technology	2.5	1.5	2.1	−2.4
Low-technology	1.0	0.0	−0.8	−4.2
Value added[b]				
High-technology	5.7	4.9	3.9	n.a.
Low-technology	3.2	1.8	0.0	n.a.
Productivity[c]				
High-technology	3.1	3.4	1.7	n.a.
Low-technology	2.2	1.9	0.8	n.a.

Sources: Same as table 4-6.
n.a. Not available.
a. Compounded annually.
b. In 1972 dollars.
c. Value added divided by employment.

has been quite similar to the productivity slump elsewhere in manufacturing, and the value-added deflators for high-technology products have not fallen relative to those of manufacturing in general.[17] Thus it is doubtful that faster technological change is the explanation.

What other explanations might account for the relatively strong output gains in high-technology products during 1973–80? One might be the relatively high income elasticity of demand for these products and the low income elasticity of demand for commodities with older traditions. Wealthy consumers devote declining shares of their incomes to basic needs such as clothing, footwear, furniture, and simple electrical appliances. Conversely, they increase the share devoted to computers, aircraft, and communications equipment. Thus, with the expansion of income, basic needs commodities can be expected to have declining shares. But if income elasticities have the dominant effect, the share of high-technology industries increases more rapidly in periods of high rather than low income growth.[18]

17. When compared with the overall rise in unit value added for manufactured goods, the natural-resource industries had increases of 49 percent in relative unit value added from 1972 to 1980, but both capital-intensive and high-technology products declined about 9 percent and labor-intensive products, 15 percent.
18. If, for example, income growth rates were infinite, commodities with elasticities of less than 1.0 would tend to have zero shares; if growth were zero, shares would remain constant. Thus the more rapid is the growth rate, the faster is the expansion of the shares of products with high income elasticities.

Perhaps, however, it is precisely because income effects have been o small during this period that the share of high-technology products as grown.[19] In explaining the demand for a product, it is customary to distinguish between income and substitution effects. In the absence of price declines, because the qualitative nature of standardized commodities changes very little, the markets for them only expand in the face of income growth. Thus under depressed cyclical conditions the demand for the products of U.S. industries such as textiles, iron and steel, other basic metals, fabricated metal products, and automobiles is particularly sluggish. On the other hand, income growth is likely to be less important as a determinant of the demand for a new product. It might be possible to increase the output of Sony Walkman radio-earphone sets in the midst of a recession, for example, whereas it is not possible to raise the output of conventional portable radios. Substitution effects due to quality changes are likely to dominate income effects. Another source of substitution effects over this period could be the demand for more energy-efficient products.[20] The close correspondence between the high-technology and the equipment groupings are suggestive of possibilities along these lines (see table A-2).

Trade

The five-year averages of the major components of the current account shown in figure 4-1 reveal the strength and persistence of trends in the composition of U.S. trade. In almost every case the curves move continuously in one direction, rising steadily for foods, feeds, and beverages, chemicals, and capital goods and services, but falling steadily for consumer goods, automobiles, and fuels and lubricants.

19. I tested a second variant of the income elasticity argument without much success. This would link the composition of manufacturing ouput to changes in the overall composition of final demand—specifically to the dramatic increase in the size of the services sector. The secular shift toward a service economy has continued at a relatively higher rate over the 1973–80 period. Of course, given the relatively slower secular rise in service industry productivity, this led to relatively faster increases in the employment share in services. If high-technology manufactured inputs are strongly complementary to services output, a shift toward services might be associated with a shift *within manufacturing* toward high-technology products and away from basic industries. Services are actually relatively more intensive in both natural resource-intensive (Ricardo) goods and capital-intensive goods than they are in high-technology goods.

20. This possibility would be compatible with Martin Neil Baily's argument that events since 1973 have led to the premature retirement of capital. See "Productivity and the Services of Capital and Labor," *Brookings Papers on Economic Activity, 1:1981,* pp. 1–50.

Figure 4-1. *Patterns in the U.S. Trade Balance, Selected Manufactured Products, 1950–82*[a]

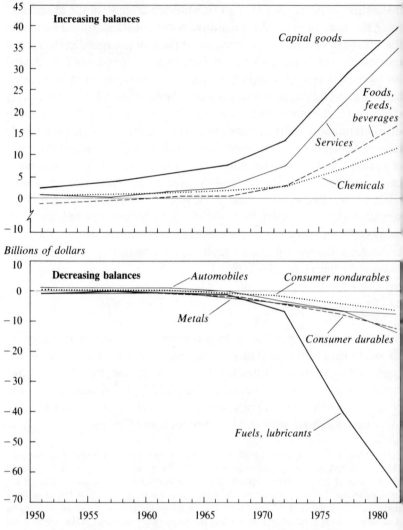

Billions of dollars

Billions of dollars

Sources: U.S. Department of Commerce, Office of Business Economics, *U.S. Exports and Imports Classified by OBE End-Use Commodity Categories, 1923–1968* (U.S. Government Printing Office, 1970); Department of Commerce, Bureau of Economic Analysis, *U.S. Merchandise Trade, Exports and Imports—1965–76, Classified by BEA End-Use Commodity Categories* (GPO, 1977); and *Survey of Current Business*, vol. 63 (June 1983).
   a. Five-year averages.

Factor Endowments

The Hecksher-Ohlin theory of trade predicts that an economy will specialize in the production of commodities that require the relatively intensive application of its more abundant factors of production. Empirical applications of the theory have been moderately successful in explaining the composition of U.S. trade at particular points in time. U.S. trade surpluses occur in commodities made with the relatively abundant factors of production—land (food) and skilled and highly educated labor (chemicals, capital goods, and services); U.S. trade deficits are in commodities made with unskilled labor (nondurable consumer goods) or requiring resources that have been depleted (fuels). It is more difficult to identify the contribution of physical capital in calculating U.S. comparative advantage.[21] As Branson has observed, 'Physical capital plays a more neutral role, combining relatively more with human capital in exports and unskilled labor [and natural resources] in imports. Good examples may be chemicals on the export side and consumer electronics [and steel] on the import side.''[22]

The theory also helps explain changes in U.S. specialization patterns over time. As foreign economies have grown more rapidly than the U.S. economy and as they have had higher ratios of investment to GNP, the U.S. share of the global capital stock has declined markedly. However, the U.S. share of skilled labor has decreased relatively little, and its

21. The debate about the role of capital goes back as far as Leontief's famous 1953 article, which found the United States exporting goods embodying labor and importing goods embodying capital. See Wassily W. Leontief, "Domestic Production and Foreign Trade: The American Capital Position Reexamined," *Proceedings of the American Philosophical Society,* vol. 97 (Philadelphia: 1953), pp. 332–49. Surveys of subsequent efforts to explain Leontief's findings are found in James C. Hartigan, "The United States Tariff and Comparative Advantage, A Survey of Method," *Weltwirtschaftliches Archiv,* vol. 117, no. 1 (1981), pp. 65–109. See also Robert M. Stern, "Testing Trade Theories," in Peter B. Kenen, *International Trade and Finance: Frontiers for Research* (Cambridge University, 1975), pp. 3–50.

22. See William H. Branson, "Trends in U.S. International Trade and Investment since World War II," in Martin Feldstein, ed., *The American Economy in Transition* (University of Chicago Press, 1980), p. 236. For a comprehensive survey of general studies on this subject see Stern, "Testing Trade Theories."

23. Bowen has calculated that the U.S. share of global supplies of capital declined from 42 percent in 1963 to 33 percent in 1975), while the share of skilled labor declined by much less (from 29 to 26 percent), and the U.S. share of global arable land actually increased (from 27 to 29 percent). See Harry P. Bowen, "Shifts in the International Distribution of Resources and the Impact of U.S. Comparative Advantage," *Review of Economics and Statistics* (forthcoming).

share of global arable land has actually increased.[23] These changes in relative factor endowments are therefore consistent with increased U.S. specialization in products that are intensive in skilled labor and land and decreased specialization in capital-intensive products.[24]

Technological Change and Economies of Scale

A less formal but more dynamic explanation of the pattern of U.S. trade incorporates the role of changes in relative technological and production capabilities and the growth of economies of scale that accompanied the convergence of foreign nations toward U.S. productivity levels. In the early 1950s the United States dominated global manufacturing capacity. In 1950 the United States produced about 60 percent of world manufactured goods output, and in 1953 it accounted for about 29 percent of manufactured goods exports. In almost every field U.S. firms stood at the technological frontier and enjoyed the economies of scale resulting from access to a large, integrated, and extremely wealthy market. U.S. inventors had devised products primarily with the view of saving labor, and as foreign productivity levels increased and real wages rose, these products became increasingly attractive abroad. In addition, World War II stimulated technological advances in computers, aircraft, and pharmaceuticals, and while it severely damaged civilian production facilities abroad, in the United States the capital stock remained intact.

The shortage of foreign manufacturing capacity can be inferred from the surpluses in the U.S. balance of trade in all major end-use categories in 1950, including those in which the United States had deficits before the war.[25] Industrialization abroad boosted the U.S. balance of trade in capital goods and chemicals, but by the late 1950s the rebuilding of Europe and the expansion of Japanese exports of textiles eroded the trade surpluses in semimanufactured goods and consumer products. In the mid-1960s foreign steel and automobiles were penetrating the U.S. market in substantial quantities, and the trade balances in semimanufactured products and automobiles became negative. As U.S. imports from the developed nations moved up the technology spectrum, the devel-

24. Stern and Maskus report that in a series of annual regressions explaining trade the coefficient on unskilled labor becomes increasingly statistically significant over time and the coefficient on capital, increasingly negative. See Stern and Maskus, "Determinants of the Structure of U.S. Foreign Trade, 1958–76."

25. See William H. Branson and Helen B. Junz, "Trends in U.S. Trade and Comparative Advantage," *Brookings Papers on Economic Activity*, 2:1971, pp. 285–338.

oping nations began to enter the market and make up increasing shares of U.S. imports of standardized labor-intensive consumer products.

On the one hand, the range of U.S. imports broadened to mirror the different stages of development of its trading partners—with labor-intensive imports originating in developing nations and capital-intensive and high-technology products originating in the industrial economies. On the other hand, the range of U.S. exports narrowed, and it became increasingly confined to capital goods, chemical and agricultural products, and services.

In the 1970s this process of U.S. specialization continued. The trade between developing nations and the United States evolved along the lines of comparative advantage associated with factor endowments related to different stages of development. However, production and technological capabilities of foreign industrial countries converged toward those of the United States, and those countries now compete with U.S. firms in high-technology products.[26] Another factor that helped close the gap in capabilities was the absence in the U.S. market of unique opportunities for American firms to realize economies of scale.[27] Indeed, foreign innovations that are directed primarily toward saving raw materials (small automobiles, for example) have become increasingly attractive to American consumers.[28]

Role of R&D

The literature disputes the precise sources of the U.S. advantage in high-technology manufactured goods. Does it result from the relative abundance of engineers and scientists, the relatively large amounts spent

26. For a detailed analysis of U.S. trade in high-technology products see C. Michael Aho and Howard F. Rosen, "Trends in Technology-Intensive Trade," Economic Discussion Paper 11 (Office of Foreign Economic Research, U.S. Department of Labor, 1980); Jack Baranson and Harald B. Malmgren, "Technology and Trade Policy: Issues and an Agenda for Action," paper prepared for the Bureau of International Labor Affairs, Department of Labor, and the Office of the U.S. Trade Representative Washington, D.C., 1981); and Sumiye Okubo, "The Impact of Technology Transfer on the Competitiveness of U.S. Producers," in *Report of the President on U.S. Competitiveness* (Office of Foreign Economic Research, U.S. Department of Labor, September 1980).

27. This is confirmed in C. Michael Aho and Richard D. Carney, "An Empirical Analysis of the Structure of U.S. Manufacturing Trade, 1964–1976," Economic Discussion Paper 3 (Bureau of International Labor Affairs, Department of Labor, June 1979).

28. See Raymond Vernon, "Gone Are the Cash Cows of Yesteryear," *Harvard Business Review*, vol. 58 (November–December 1980), pp. 150–55.

on R&D, or the market inducements to innovate in a rich economy? The strong interactions among these possibilities inhibit quantifying the contribution of each.[29] However, it is possible to provide a snapshot of the kinds of manufactured goods the United States succeeds in exporting and those in which import penetration has been the greatest.

U.S. export industries have made large investments in R&D and are at the technological frontier.[30] The products are often novel, require specialized production methods, and benefit during their development from being close to the market in which they are sold. Staying ahead requires continual innovation to offset the inevitable standardization of the production process and the international diffusion of technology. Conversely, U.S. imports, especially those from developing countries, are by and large mature and standardized products that can be mass-produced using quickly acquired skills. They may be manufactured products requiring unskilled labor (such as apparel and footwear) or products that rely upon capital relatively intensively (such as steel).

The growing importance of high-technology trade to the United States is illustrated by figure 4-2, which contrasts the U.S. trade balances in R&D and non-R&D-intensive products.[31] The geographic distribution of the U.S. trade balances in R&D-intensive products corresponds to the relative stage of development of U.S. trading partners. Thus, as illustrated in figure 4-3, the United States has sustained a large and growing surplus in R&D-intensive products with the developing countries and with Europe, while its trade in these products with Germany has remained in rough balance and with Japan it has moved toward a growing deficit.

Conclusion

In summary, the effect of trade has not been to shrink the U.S. manufacturing sector, and the United States has not lost its comparative

29. On this question see Thomas C. Lowinger, "The Technology Factor and the Export Performance of U.S. Manufacturing Industries," *Economic Inquiry,* vol. 3 (June 1975), pp. 221–36.

30. The classic generalization along these lines is Vernon's product-cycle theory. See Raymond Vernon, "International Investment and International Trade in the Product Cycle," *Quarterly Journal of Economics,* vol. 80 (May 1966), pp. 190–207.

31. The United States has maintained its share in world trade of high-technology products far better than in more routine goods. See Bela Balassa, "U.S. Export Performance: A Trade Share Analysis," Working Papers in Economics 24 (Baltimore, Md.: Johns Hopkins University, May 1977).

Figure 4-2. *U.S. Trade Balance in R&D-intensive and Non-R&D-intensive Manufactured Products, 1960–80*[a]

Billions of dollars

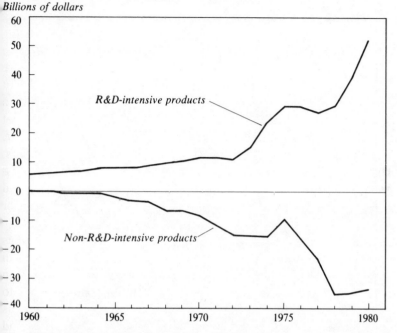

Source: National Science Foundation, *Science Indicators 1982* (GPO, 1983), p. 21.
a. Exports minus imports.

advantage in manufacturing as a whole. The United States has been developing a growing comparative advantage in high-technology and resource-intensive products, while its comparative advantage in labor-intensive and capital-intensive products manufactured with standardized technologies has been eroding. There is, therefore, a correspondence between the U.S. industries experiencing slow economic growth because of sluggish domestic use and those experiencing declining comparative advantage.

The direction of structural change in U.S. domestic markets and in U.S. comparative advantage may well be causally linked. The shift toward the demand for high-technology products domestically may be an important source of the growth in comparative advantage of the United States in these products; and conversely, the shifts away from older, more traditional products may have contributed to their relative decline. Burenstam Linder stresses the availability of markets and associated scale-economies rather than of factors of production such as

Figure 4-3. *U.S. Trade Balance in R&D-intensive Manufactured
Products, Selected Countries, 1966–80*[a]

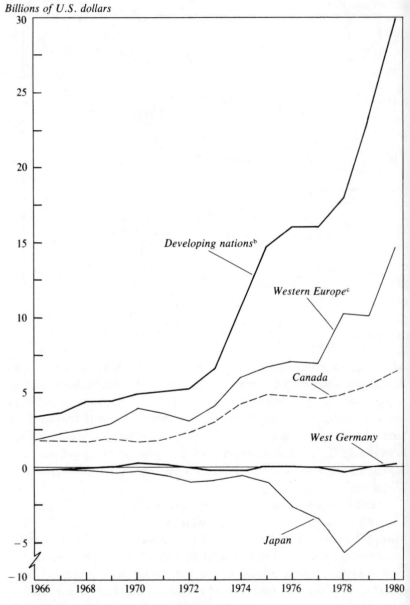

Billions of U.S. dollars

Source: National Science Foundation, *Science Indicators 1982*, p. 22.
a. Exports minus imports.
b. Includes the Republic of South Africa in 1966 and 1967.
c. Includes West Germany.

capital or labor as the major determinant of comparative advantage and expresses the view that countries should export goods that are demanded in their home markets.[32] Linder notes that a country typically exports goods that fit the standard of living attained by a large number of its population. Thus the United States may export jet aircraft, for example, because the substantial domestic demand for these products has provided the incentive for producers to manufacture such aircraft. Upon entering production, these U.S. producers have enjoyed advances in productivity through learning-by-doing and by exploiting economies of scale in production that allow them to compete effectively abroad. Similarly, producers in Japan successfully sell abroad the small cars demanded by its domestic market.

Characteristics of High- and Low-Growth Industries

Would the current job losers from the low-technology industries be employable in high-technology industries? To some degree, those displaced will find employment in other sectors of the economy. The issue of structural mismatch across manufacturing remains, however. In particular, there has been concern about the distributional effects of changes in the structure of U.S. manufacturing.[33]

Employment Growth and High Technology

Some major characteristics of workers in high- and low-technology industries are shown in table 4-10. An examination of the averages reported in the table suggests differences that might be expected; workers in high-technology industries tend to be more highly paid, better educated, male, white, relatively young, and less unionized than their low-technology counterparts.[34] The differences in regional location and occupational characteristics between high- and low-technology workers

32. Staffan Burenstam Linder, *An Essay on Trade and Transformation* (Wiley, 1961).
33. On the effects of trade, see Aho and Carney, "An Empirical Analysis of the Structure of U.S. Manufacturing Trade, 1961–1976."
34. The high-technology products tend to have lower ratios of physical capital per employee. This has an important link to the Leontief paradox discussed above.

Table 4-10. *Some Characteristics of U.S. Manufacturing, High- and Low-Technology Industries, Computers, Automobiles, and the Steel Industry during the Past Two Decades*[a]

Percent unless otherwise specified

Item	High-technology industry	Low-technology industry	Computers	Automobiles	Steel
Employees (thousands)[b]	6,513.4	13,771.6	354.2	788.8	428.4
Black employees[c]	5.3	9.7	4.1	13.5	13.0
Women employees[b]	30.7	33.2	35.9	14.0	6.9
Production workers[b]	62.1	74.3	40.0	72.9	77.5
Employees covered by collective bargaining[d]					
All workers	38.9	49.0	11.0	72.0	77.0
Production workers	58.2	61.5	15.0	98.0	98.0
Median number of school years completed[c]	12.5	11.6	13.7	12.1	12.0
Median age in years[c]	38.9	40.3	32.6	39.3	43.7
Work force stability (percent of workers employed 50–52 weeks)[c]	76.8	70.4	79.5	70.9	77.8
Average hourly wage of production workers (dollars)[b]	7.62	7.12	6.73	9.85	11.84
Average annual compensation of all workers (dollars)[b]	22,300	18,800	23,000	30,300	34,100
Capital-labor ratio (dollars)[b]	23,700	30,790	21,600	40,200	93,400
Labor's share[b]	51.9	50.3	47.7	70.8	73.8
Large-plant percentage[e]	41.4	23.6	58.5	71.5	89.4
Concentration ratio[e]	42.8	36.4	44.0	82.0	45.0
Allocation of employment by geographic census regions[f]					
Middle Atlantic	21.4	20.5	18.6	8.8	32.9
New England	10.0	6.6	12.1	1.2	0.4
East North Central	28.8	24.7	4.6	65.9	42.7
West North Central	6.2	6.0	14.0	6.7	1.3
South	19.6	32.1	13.4	11.5	16.5
West	14.0	10.1	37.3	6.0	6.1

Sources: Annual compensation, capital-labor ratio, and share of labor are from U.S. Bureau of the Census, *1980 Annual Survey of Manufactures*, M80 (A5)-5 (September 1982); race, school years, age, and work force stability are from Bureau of the Census, *1970 Census of Population* (U.S. Government Printing Office, 1973); concentration ratios and regional employment are from Bureau of the Census, *1972 Census of Manufactures* (GPO, 1975) and *1977 Census of Manufactures* (GPO, 1981), respectively; data on total employment, women, production workers, and average wages are from Bureau of Labor Statistics, *Employment and Earnings*, various issues; union coverage is from Richard B. Freeman and James L. Medoff, "New Estimates of Private Sector Unionism in the United States," *Industrial and Labor Relations Review*, vol. 32 (January 1979), pp. 143–74.

n.a. Not available.

a. The characteristics of high- and low-technology industries are based on a sample of three-digit 1970 census code industries that employed 85 percent of the employees in manufacturing in 1980. Employment figures for high- and low-technology industries are from total manufacturing data. The SIC codes for computers, automobiles, and steel are 3573, 371, and 3312, respectively.

b. In 1980. Annual compensation includes social security and benefits. The capital-labor ratio is the gross book value of depreciable assets divided by employment. Labor's share is total employee compensation divided by value added.

c. In 1970. To derive median school years and median age I computed the weighted average (by number of employees) of the medians of men and women in the three-digit 1970 census-code industries.

d. From surveys of the 1968–72 period.

e. In 1977. The concentration ratio is the weighted average of the percent of output produced by the four largest companies in each four-digit SIC industry. The large-plant percentage is the percent of employees in establishments with 1,000 or more workers.

f. In 1972; Bureau of Census regions.

generally are surprisingly small.[35] This suggests that most of the workers could be employed in either sector.

The common perceptions of the structural adjustment problem are not captured by the aggregate numbers but are again heavily influenced by the characteristics of a few prominent industries. Some striking differences can be seen when one compares characteristics of the steel and automobile industries with those of the computer industry, as reported in table 4-10. The greater visibility and political influence of the steel and automobile industries have perhaps exaggerated their importance. First, these are industries traditionally and perhaps anachronistically associated with industrial prowess. Second, automobiles in particular are viewed as an important source of employment and demand in other industries—for example, in 1972 the total direct and indirect employment relating to U.S. motor vehicle production amounted to almost 10 percent of total employment in U.S. manufacturing.[36] Third, these industries operate large plants; they are concentrated in specific regions (in 1972, 66 percent of U.S. automobile employment was in the East North Central census region and 76 percent of steel employment in the East North Central and Middle Atlantic regions); and they are heavily unionized. Fourth, both employers and employees have considerable financial incentives to resist change. Workers earn large wage premiums that reflect advantages such as seniority benefits, monopoly rents, and the support of strong unions that they would not receive if employed elsewhere.[37] And last, employers in these industries have invested unusually large amounts of capital per worker.

In most of these respects the computer industry is strikingly different. Its work force has considerably more white, female, educated, and young workers; it is much less unionized and is heavily concentrated in the western part of the United States. Thus if the "structural problem" of the reemployment of U.S. labor involves hiring automobile workers

35. Except for race. For an analysis of the employment effects of trade on minorities see Robert Z. Lawrence, "Minority Employment and U.S. Trade," in *Foreign Trade Policy and Black Economic Advancement* (Washington, D.C.: Joint Center for Political Studies, 1981), pp. 49–62.

36. According to the Bureau of Labor Statistics, employment in the automobile industry itself comprised 4.6 percent of employment in manufacturing in 1972. Using input-output analysis, I estimate that output in the automobile industry indirectly generated employment in the rest of manufacturing, and thus accounted for an additional 4.9 percent.

37. Compensation in steel and automobiles in 1980 was 53 percent and 36 percent higher, respectively, than in high-technology industries.

to build computers, as conventional wisdom appears to presume, the problem appears considerable. If, however, it involves a gradual replace ment of low-technology jobs with high-technology jobs, it seems far more manageable. Considering that in November 1982 unemployed workers from primary metals and automobiles, many of whom were likely to be recalled, constituted, respectively, about 2.5 and 2.1 percent of total U.S. unemployment (and 9.1 and 7.7 percent of unemployment in manufacturing), the problems for these industries, while substantial for the individuals and firms involved, were a relatively small part of the overall story of U.S. manufacturing.[38]

The Disappearing Middle?

Some believe that there are fewer opportunities to earn "middle class" incomes in the high-technology sectors than in the rest of manufacturing.[39] I tested this hypothesis by defining middle-class jobs as those within a range of 30 percent above and 30 percent below the median male income in the economy and analyzed data from the 1970 census on earnings of the experienced work force by industry.[40] The data do not support this belief. In 1969, 44.6 percent of workers in manufacturing earned middle-class incomes while 47 percent of workers in high-technology manufacturing earned middle-class incomes.[41]

Since manufacturing, in general, has a higher proportion of middle class jobs than the rest of the economy, a decline in manufacturing is likely to be associated with a decline in the availability of such jobs.[42] In

38. In 1980 U.S. employment in motor vehicles and equipment (SIC 371) and in primary iron and steel manufacturing (SIC 331) amounted to 788,800 and 511,900 respectively, and was 6.4 percent of manufacturing employment. Together these industries accounted for about 14.1 percent of the 1,432,000 decline in U.S. manufacturing employment from 1980 to 1982.

39. According to Lester Thurow, for example, "Part of the change in (U.S.) income distribution is due to the characteristics of America's new growth industries. High technology industries such as microelectronics tend to have two levels of income distributions—high and low—as opposed to the smokestack industries." See "The Disappearance of the Middle Class," *New York Times*, February 5, 1984.

40. I use this approximation because the data are only provided in discrete categories

41. In 1979, according to preliminary census data, these proportions were 39.3 and 41.8 percent, respectively. Thus the proportion of middle-class jobs in U.S. manufacturing is declining, but shifts in the mix between high- and low-technology do not explain this decline.

42. See, for example, Robert Kuttner, "The Declining Middle," *Atlantic Monthly*, vol. 252 (July 1983), pp. 60–72.

1969, for example, middle-class jobs were about 44.6 percent of all jobs in manufacturing, and 34.8 percent of all jobs in the rest of the economy. Given that the manufacturing sector's share of total employment was 26.4 percent, a decline in that sector is unlikely to have a major impact on the overall income distribution in the United States. If sectors having the same proportion of middle-class jobs as the rest of the economy (34.8 percent) replaced the entire U.S. manufacturing sector, the total number of middle-class jobs available in the United States would decline by 7.4 percent.[43]

Structural Change and Employment

Under normal circumstances employment shifts due to structural change should be easily accomplished by the U.S. economy. If one takes the changes over the 1970s as indicating the magnitude of secular structural shifts, for most declining industries the annual average employment drop is rather small. Taken together, employment in industries that do not depend on high technology fell at an annual average rate of 0.03 percent in the 1970s, while the decline from the cyclical peak in 1973 through the more slack conditions in 1980 averaged 0.79 percent a year. In fact, the employment loss due to the shift in structural change over the entire decade of the 1970s was considerably smaller than the drop in any one year of a major recession. For example, from 1973 to 1975 the employment in low-technology industries fell at an annual average rate of 5.3 percent while from 1979 to 1982 the drop averaged 4.3 percent a year.

To be sure, in some industries the pace of decline over the decade was more rapid. In wood containers and leather products—the sectors with the greatest employment loss over this period—the declines averaged 3.3 and 2.4 percent a year, respectively. Yet considering the typical rate at which workers voluntarily quit their jobs, even these industries would be able to cope with a smooth declining employment trend without involuntary layoffs. The problem, of course, is that such changes do not occur smoothly; they coincide with the business cycle and may take the form of sporadic plant closures rather than smooth exponential decay.

43. According to preliminary census data, the decline in the share of male employment in U.S. manufacturing between 1969 and 1979 can account for less than half of 1 percent of the total decline in middle-class jobs available to U.S. males in the economy over the period.

The real nature of the structural adjustment problem facing U.S. industry cannot be captured by the aggregate numbers. It lies rather in the characteristics of the declining industries that tend to increase their visibility and improve their political clout. Four of the five two-digit industries with the slowest employment growth (tobacco, automobiles, primary metals, and textiles) are among the top five U.S. industries ranked by plant size—and their plants are often important for the economic health of the regions in which they are located. Moreover, workers in steel and automobiles earn wage premiums that reflect benefits such as seniority, monopoly rents, and the influence of strong unions— benefits that such workers would not enjoy if they were employed elsewhere. They have, therefore, considerable financial incentives to resist structural change. Trade intervention is frequently the only way policymakers can show their concern. Yet as the analysis above indicates, trade is rarely the major reason for the decline.

Much has been made of the structural nature of the unemployment in U.S. manufacturing during 1980–82. It is commonly argued that the jobs lost in the current recession in basic industries will not be replaced even if the economy recovers strongly. But with a return of the exchange rate to near its 1980 level and a recovery of the economy, there is no reason to believe this. As I argued above, it is normal in a recession for high-technology employment to decline less rapidly than employment in the rest of manufacturing. From 1979 to 1982, employment in high-technology industries fell about 3.4 percent a year less rapidly than the rest of manufacturing—a differential that was remarkably similar to that in 1973–75. The 1.8 percent differential that occurred in 1980–82 was quite similar to the 1.6 percent differential for the 1970s as a whole.

Regressions of employment in high- and low-technology industries against a time trend and capacity utilization in manufacturing over the 1970s indicate a slight upward long-run trend for low-technology employment of about 0.2 percent a year and an increase of about 1.8 percent a year for high-technology employment. Had capacity utilization been at its 1970–80 average, employment in 1982 in high- and low-technology industries would have been higher by 260,000 and 1.5 million, respectively. A more competitive value of the dollar would have added still more to employment, as already noted.

A return to the long-run employment trend by 1990 would entail average annual employment gains during 1982–90 of 2.5 percent and 1.5

percent a year in high- and low-technology manufacturing, respectively. In summary, employment in manufacturing has fallen considerably below its long-run trend. Given reasonable economic expansion and international price competitiveness, structural change should now be relatively easy to accommodate in the remainder of the 1980s.

Policy Options

CHAPTER FIVE

The Questionable Case
for Selective Industrial Policies

IN previous chapters I suggested that slow overall growth in the economy and a strong currency appear to be the dominant reasons for the adjustment problems facing U.S. manufacturing. An alteration of U.S. macroeconomic policies could contribute significantly toward ameliorating these difficulties.

The United States could change its macroeconomic policies to make foreign markets more attractive to U.S. firms; these policies and those of other industrial countries have exacerbated the structural adjustment problems facing the world economy. Since inflation restraint remains a major policy objective, it is likely that the United States will pursue a relatively restrained overall thrust to aggregate demand policy over the next few years. But the monetary and fiscal policy mix on which policymakers rely to achieve any given level of demand will have an important influence on international competitiveness.

The U.S. budget deficit and current account deficit can be directly linked. If the economy is at full employment, and the government seeks to increase its consumption, either the private sector will have to consume less or the goods will have to be obtained from abroad. Thus in the absence of a change in private spending patterns, a greater government deficit at full employment will lead to a greater trade deficit. As the U.S. government borrows, interest rates rise. These higher interest rates induce capital inflows, which strengthen the dollar. This makes domestic products expensive, reduces the trade balance, and diverts investment from firms competing in international trade, both at home and abroad. Given private spending behavior, an increase in the government deficit thus leads to an increase in the trade deficit. High interest rates also adversely affect domestic investment unless tax relief to firms offsets this effect.

A preferable strategy, some believe, is to reduce U.S. interest rates through tighter long-run fiscal policy (requiring lower spending, especially on defense, and higher taxes) in return for a relatively easier monetary policy. These policies would entail lower interest rates, reduce capital inflows and, since a smaller government deficit implies less need to absorb foreign resources, result in a weaker dollar. An improvement in international competitiveness obtained in this manner would mean more stimulus to the economy from the foreign sector and less from the government sector. It would channel investment toward all U.S. firms competing in foreign trade. The policy would be even more effective if coordinated with moves by the Japanese and others to change their policy mix toward looser fiscal and somewhat tighter monetary policies.

The United States has many structural policies. Some of these are general in nature, such as policies pertaining to the rules of domestic competition (mergers and antitrust laws) and international competition (antidumping laws) and policies facilitating the adjustment of factors of production (worker training and placement, capital formation, and R&D). Other policies are specific to sectors; examples are energy, agricultural, and housing policies.

Because structural policies are widespread, the real issue is not whether the United States needs industrial policies but rather how existing policies can be made more effective. Although this study has questioned the existence of many of the problems alleged to plague U.S. industry, it should not be assumed that current U.S. structural programs leave no room for improvement.

A new set of proposals, labeled industrial policy, is currently attracting much attention. Proponents seek a fundamental change in the way in which resources are allocated in the U.S. economy. Two advocates of such an approach, Magaziner and Reich, have suggested that "U.S. companies and the government develop a coherent and coordinated industrial policy whose aim is to raise the real income of our citizens by improving the patterns of our investments rather than by focusing only on aggregate investment levels."[1] The novelty in these views is the notion that U.S. structural policies should be explicitly selective and that the government should develop a conception of the direction in which the economy should evolve. Employing a wide range of instru-

---

1. Ira C. Magaziner and Robert B. Reich, *Minding America's Business: The Decline and Rise of the American Economy* (Harcourt Brace Jovanovich, 1982), p. 4.

ments, the government, so the argument goes, channels resources in that direction. Preferred sectors are aided with government loans and equity participation, trade protection and export subsidies, government procurement, and relief from regulatory constraints such as antitrust and environmental laws. Aid may depend on commitments by the industry to reduce wages, maintain employment, reform work rules, locate in depressed regions, and increase investment. Policy is coordinated by tripartite councils with members from business, labor, and government.

Proponents of such policies are divided on the issue of which sectors should receive help. Advocates of the *defensive* approach seek to aid troubled "sunset" industries such as steel, automobiles, glass, rubber, and other basic industries. Their aim is to retard the pace and reverse the pattern of structural change. As Rohatyn sees it, "what we have to do is to turn the losers into winners, restructure our basic industries to make them competitive and use whatever U.S. government resources are necessary to do the job."[2] Advocates of the *offensive* approach seek to focus on "sunrise" industries—those with the greatest potential for growth and international competitiveness.

As even their proponents acknowledge, these selective industrial policies require considerable time to take effect; design, implementation, operation, and evaluation impose long lags. Selective policies are also costly to consumers and to taxpayers. Because they confer benefits on powerful domestic interests, they are probably irreversible. Also, nations abroad might emulate selective policy of the United States, with the accompanying risk of a rise in global levels of protection. It is crucial, therefore, that proponents provide a plan that (1) focuses on permanent trends and not transitory shifts due to business-cycle or exchange-rate fluctuations for which monetary and fiscal policies are more appropriate tools, (2) in principle has the potential to improve resource allocation, and (3) in practice improves resource allocation if implemented in the U.S. political and institutional context.

In this chapter, I consider three questions: How accurate is the empirical case for selective industrial policies? How suitable are the criteria and methods by which resources would be allocated by such policies? And could such policies be effectively implemented in the United States?

2. Felix Rohatyn, "Reconstructing America," *New York Review of Books* (March 5, 1981), p. 16.

The Empirical Case

The case for selective industrial policy is based upon some widely shared perceptions about U.S. manufacturing performance. A stylized version of the argument is as follows. There are fundamental deficiencies in the U.S. industrial system. Americans fail to produce quality goods because managers are myopic and care only about short-term profits. Workers lack discipline and are shackled by work rules, and labor and management look on one another as adversaries. U.S. government policy is also to blame. Trade protection, granted unconditionally, has slowed adjustment to international competition. The government has failed to plan and coordinate its industrial evolution. It ought to have policies that promote industries with potential and assist those in decline. It ought to have a lending institution, operated by the government, to provide "patient capital" for long-term investments ignored by the market.

Foreign industrial economies have avoided these American problems. Abroad, management has patiently plowed resources into new plant, equipment, and research and development. Governments have consciously followed adjustment policies, which have successfully channeled resources away from declining industries and into those with long-run growth potential. They have also pursued social policies that have encouraged cooperative attitudes between labor and management. The result: productivity growth abroad has far outpaced that in the United States. As Robert Reich argues, "America's relative decline has been rooted in changes in the world market . . . Japan, West Germany, and France and other industrialized countries have been shifting their industrial bases toward products and processes that require skilled labor. . . . America's evolution has so far been sluggish."[3]

Growing international competition has sharpened the contrast between U.S. deficiencies and foreign prowess. U.S. industry has lost its lead in manufactured products across the board. As Lester Thurow sees it, "What is going on is not a normal 'product cycle' where high-technology, high-wage products are introduced in America but gradually become low-technology, low-wage products that can best be produced

3. See Robert B. Reich, *The Next American Frontier* (New York Times Books, 1983), pp. 121–33.

abroad. America is being whipped on the tail end of the economy, but it is also being whipped on the front end of the economy."[4]

In the developing countries in particular, advances in automation have allowed producers to equip their low-wage work forces with the most modern machinery and to become highly competitive in consumer electronics, shipbuilding, steel, textiles, and consumer goods. In the developed economies, producers sheltered by trade protection and aided by government subsidies can compete with the high-technology products of the United States.

Exchange rates cannot offset the effects of the foreign subsidies and trade protection, and foreign trade has therefore resulted in the broad erosion of U.S. industrial employment and, indeed, threatens to deindustrialize America. The U.S. industrial base has eroded precipitously. The economy has experienced unprecedented turbulence as a result of trade and is becoming increasingly specialized in agriculture and services.

This transition from manufacturing entails immense dislocation and has major consequences for the survival of the United States as an economic power. According to Thurow, "Like it or not, if American manufacturing goes down the tubes, most of the rest of us will go down with it."[5] To avoid the fate of deindustrialization and to reverse the current patterns of structural change, the United States must therefore respond with selective industrial policies of its own.

Evidence from the Manufacturing Sector

As I have shown in the preceding chapters, many of the perceptions about U.S. manufacturing are inaccurate, and it is on these perceptions that the empirical case for selective industrial policies rests. Consider the evidence discussed above from the latter part of the 1970s in which the forces allegedly damaging the U.S. industrial base were already present—surging competition from the developing countries and Japan and protection in Europe. Compared with past U.S. rates or those of other major industrial countries, manufacturing industries in the United States did not fail to invest in physical capital or in R&D.

Since 1973, compared with other major industrial countries, U.S. employment growth in manufacturing was unusually strong, and com-

4. Lester C. Thurow, "The Case for Industrial Policies" (1983), p. 5.
5. Ibid., p. 7.

pared with Germany and Japan the new U.S. jobs were disproportionately in industries with high growth potential. U.S. investment has also
moved increasingly toward these high-technology sectors. Productivity
growth in U.S. manufacturing declined after 1973, but as Gollop has
demonstrated, sectoral shifts within manufacturing have been unimportant in explaining the slowdown in aggregate productivity growth. Thus
there is no evidence that a superior allocation of resources among U.S.
industries could have avoided the slowdown.[6] In short, U.S. manufacturing shortcomings stem neither from a failure to commit resources to
manufacturing nor from a failure to reallocate manufacturing inputs.

In fact, America is not deindustrializing. From 1950 to 1973 U.S.
production of manufactured goods grew as rapidly as GNP. Productivity
growth was faster in manufacturing than in the rest of the economy,
however, so the *share* of employment in manufacturing declined. After
1973 the output in manufacturing grew more slowly than the GNP, but
this is explained by the greater sensitivity of such output to changes in
growth. From 1973 to 1982, based on the historical relation between
industrial production and GNP, U.S. manufacturing output was predictable given the overall growth in GNP. Thus the evidence points to
demand rather than supply as the reason for recent slow growth in
manufacturing. The sluggish expansion in manufacturing output is a
global phenomenon. Indeed, since 1973 the United States has retained
its share in the OECD's production of manufactured goods. Although
manufacturing output has grown more slowly in the United States than
in Japan, the pace at which that output has grown has exceeded that of
most European economies.

Claims that the United States is deindustrializing have rested on
partial and selective evidence. Frequently figures referring to the behavior of the whole economy are erroneously used to represent the manufacturing sector. Thus the decline in the growth rate of the capital-labor
ratio in the U.S. economy as a whole has not been associated with
decline in the growth rate of the capital-labor ratio in U.S. manufacturing.
The decreasing ratio of total R&D spending to GNP that was experienced
during some periods of the 1970s is not present in the ratio of R&D to
output in manufacturing. Similarly, higher ratios of saving and invest-

6. Frank M. Gollop, "Evidence for a Sector-Biased or Sector-Neutral Industrial
Policy: Analysis of the Productivity Slowdown," Department of Economics Working
Paper 115 (Boston College, May 1982).

ment to GNP abroad are not necessarily translated into higher rates of foreign capital formation in manufacturing. Claims of the superior adjustment capabilities of other industrial economies—in particular, their ability to move workers into high-growth sectors—are based on the proclaimed goals of foreign policymakers rather than actual behavior in those economies and on anecdotal examples rather than on comprehensive data.

Some observers question whether U.S. investment has been of the right kind. It has been argued that the high dependence of U.S. corporations on equity financing induces an excessive concern for short-term profitability. The idea is that stockholders, obsessed with balance sheets and short-run profits, influence firms to pursue short-run gains. Speculators in stock markets overvalue short-term profits and undervalue long-term growth potential. Yet if this allegation is true, there is scope for investors to purchase stocks in firms with long-run potential and to hold those stocks until future profits are realized by the market. It is difficult to understand why such profit opportunities are not recognized by market participants.

Lawrence Summers suggests an empirical test for this assertion.[7] Firms with their expected earnings far in the future will tend to have high price-earnings ratios.[8] Conversely, firms with large current profits will tend to have low price-earnings ratios. If the market has a systematic tendency to undervalue the former, Summers notes, holding stocks with high price-earnings ratios should turn out to be more profitable than holding stocks with low price-earnings ratios. Drawing on the empirical studies of Basu, however, he finds no support for this contention.[9]

The Foreign Record

The numerous reviews of the foreign evidence of industrial policy do not support the view that selective policies have been crucial in the

---

7. Lawrence Summers, "Symptoms of Myopia," *New York Times*, August 5, 1983.

8. The extreme case is a firm with *all* its earnings in the future and a price-earnings ratio of infinity; a firm with all earnings in the current period would have a ratio of unity.

9. S. Basu, "Investment Performance of Common Stocks in Relation to Their Price-Earnings Ratios: A Test of the Efficient Market Hypothesis," *Journal of Finance*, vol. 32 (June 1977), pp. 663–82. See also Arthur M. Lorus, "A Random Walk through the 500," *Fortune* (May 2, 1983), pp. 267–70. In this study, between 1977 and 1982 "no significant correlation between P/E's and performance" was found.

positive industrial performance of nations abroad.[10] Most of the success stories, particularly in the case of the European economies, stem from experience before 1973. That was a period in which successful performance was apparent both in the interventionist economies such as those of Japan and France and in the free market approaches of West Germany. It was an era of unprecedented global economic growth and prosperity under conditions rather different from those of today. In addition to the different global environment, foreign economies applying the policies were at very different stages of economic development from the current U.S. level; they could absorb surplus labor, and later farm labor, equip such workers with the latest technology, and thereby enjoy great productivity gains. In recent times the European economies have demonstrated a severe inability to adapt to change, a situation frequently ascribed to precisely the types of policies that have emphasized the promotion of particular industries.[11] Japanese performance has been better, but as Saxonhouse and also Trezise have convincingly argued, Japanese industrial policies have not been the primary reason.[12]

The Role of Trade

As I showed in chapter 2, trade did not reduce aggregate employment in U.S. manufacturing during the 1970s. Aided by several devaluations, U.S. firms were able to compete from 1973 to 1980. The U.S. trade balance in manufactured products increased from a deficit of $0.3 billion to a surplus of $18.8 billion. In contrast to its declining historical trend, the share of U.S. manufactured exports in world manufactured goods exports held its own.

From 1973 to 1980, U.S. productivity growth in manufacturing was

10. Paul Krugman, "Foreign Experience with Industrial Policy" (MIT, July 1980); George C. Eads, "The Political Experience in Allocating Investment: Lessons from the United States and Elsewhere," in Michael L. Wachter and M. Susan, eds., *Toward a New U.S. Industrial Policy* (University of Pennsylvania, 1981), p. 454; Charles L. Schultze, "Industrial Policy: A Dissent," *Brookings Review*, vol. 2 (Fall 1983), pp. 3–12; and Linda Hesselman, "Trends in European Industrial Intervention," *Cambridge Journal of Economics*, vol. 7 (June 1983), pp. 197–208. For a more favorable appraisal see Magaziner and Reich, *Minding America's Business*.
11. See, for example, the essays in Rahl Dahrendorf, ed., *Europe's Economy in Crisis* (New York: Holmes & Meir, 1982).
12. Gary R. Saxonhouse, "What Is All This about Industrial Targeting in Japan?" *The World Economy*, vol. 6 (September 1983), pp. 253–274; and Philip Trezise, "Industrial Policy Is Not the Major Reason for Japan's Success," vol. 1, *Brookings Review* (Spring 1983), pp. 13–18.

slower than it was in most other industrial countries. But in the 1970s, slower rises in U.S. wages and profits and the depreciation of the dollar more than offset the slower growth in U.S. manufacturing productivity. As measured by the International Monetary Fund over the 1970s, the dollar prices of U.S. manufactured exports increased 13 percent less than the dollar prices of U.S. competitors.

All other things being equal, the slower rise in U.S. export prices, as compared with U.S. import prices, reduced U.S. welfare. In this sense, in the 1970s the U.S. lost competitiveness: to keep the current account at the same share of GNP, a lower exchange rate was required. Paying for a given volume of imports with more U.S. products resulted in an erosion of U.S. living standards but did not erode the U.S. industrial base. To the contrary, a rise in manufactured inputs was required. In short, slowing productivity growth is a serious problem from the point of view of living standards. But it is *not* a cause of decreased competitiveness in international markets.

The dominant employment gains from trade over this period came in high-technology industries in which U.S. comparative advantage continues to increase. The trade balance in products of these industries grew from $15 billion in 1973 to $52 billion in 1980.[13] As these numbers indicate, even though other industrial countries have converged toward U.S. technological capabilities and the U.S. absolute advantage in high-technology production has declined, the U.S. comparative advantage in high-technology products has actually increased. It is a failure to distinguish between absolute and comparative advantage that leads some to the erroneous conclusion that a shrinking of technological lead implies an inability to compete in international trade.

Developing countries *can* buy the latest equipment and use their low-wage workers to make some standardized products more cheaply than they can be produced in developed countries. But the machines that embody the latest equipment are built in the developed countries. Thus the process of international specialization does not lead to a loss in manufacturing in general, but rather to a decline in employment in the production of standardized products in the developed economies, which is offset by an increase in employment in more sophisticated capital goods. Indeed, the United States, with its great export concentration in machinery, has derived particular benefits from North-South trade. The rapidly growing oil-importing developing countries were the fastest

13. National Science Foundation, *Science Indicators 1982* (U.S. Government Printing Office, 1983), p. 214.

growing markets for U.S. manufactured goods. From 1973 to 1980, U.S. exports of manufactured products to these countries actually grew more rapidly than those of Japan.

The process of international specialization is therefore changing the structure of U.S. manufacturing: it is shifting employment toward high-technology industries and away from basic industries. However, trade is not the major reason for this shift. Domestic factors, such as demand patterns and technological change, have far more importance.

In summary, the evidence does not support the contention that beyond predictable consequences of a recession and the strong dollar, significant structural forces are deindustrializing America. During the 1970s, employment in manufacturing in the United States has grown and capital formation and R&D spending have proceeded at a rapid pace. The process of international specialization has reinforced domestic trends reallocating U.S. resources away from some industries and toward others, but it has done so at a pace that should not cause severe adjustment problems. To perceive trade as the major source of structural change exaggerates its role. First, changes in trade have tended to mirror the already existing domestic changes in technology and patterns of demand. Second, the influence of the strong dollar has reinforced the effects of the recent domestic recession. In the current environment, however, U.S. manufacturing does not require special new structural policies in order to compete.

The Conceptual Basis for Industrial Policies

Before evaluating the criteria and the means by which industrial policies would operate it is important to clarify what such policies can and cannot do.

Microeconomic versus Macroeconomic Policies

The industrial policy debate is about how society should allocate its resources in the long run; it is not about how to accomplish or maintain full employment. This debate should focus on how the U.S. economy can best achieve a given trade balance; not on how to increase the trade balance. Popular discussion about structural policies often alludes to their effects on the level of employment and the trade balance. But since such policies are typically microeconomic measures (such as tariffs, quotas, subsidies, taxes, loan guarantees, and government procurement) implemented over long periods of time, most of their effects will be on the *composition* of output, employment, and trade rather than on the level of employment and the trade balance.[14]

The trade balance in goods and services is by definition equal to the difference between national saving and national investment.[15] In the long run, therefore, the trade balance will reflect macroeconomic spending patterns rather than microeconomic measures such as selective industrial policies. Macroeconomic policies, rather than industrial policies, are thus the appropriate policy tools for changing the level of employment in the short run and the trade balance (or current account) in the long run. In the absence of a change in national saving and investment rates, a policy that promotes exports of high-technology products by the United States will eventually lead to greater import competition for U.S. firms. Conversely, a policy that minimizes U.S. imports will eventually lead to a reduction in U.S. exports.

These considerations have important implications for proponents of selective industrial policies. The question for those wishing to promote export of U.S. high technology products must be, Why seek to increase the competitive problems facing U.S. imports? Similarly, the question for those who would prevent foreign imports must be, Why is it desirable to increase the competitive problems facing U.S. exports? As this discussion also makes clear, however, a macroeconomic policy that reduces the proportion of U.S. income spent (by increasing saving relative to investment) could reduce the trade deficit (increase the surplus), thereby improving the competitiveness of all U.S. firms engaging in trade.

Selection Criteria

The discussion about industrial policies often implies that if the United States fails to adopt selective industrial policies, its current account can

14. There may be some exceptions. For example, certain structural policies may be designed expressly to lower the full-employment rate. See, for example, Martin Neil Baily and James Tobin, "Macroeconomic Effects of Selective Public Employment and Wage Subsidies," *Brookings Papers on Economic Activity*, 2:1977, pp. 511–41.

15. From the national income accounts, $Y = C + I + X - M$, where Y is income; C, private and government consumption spending; I, investment; X, exports; and M, imports. This can also be expressed as $Y - C - I = X - M$, that is, the current account $(X - M)$ equals the difference between income and spending on consumption plus investment. Then $S - I = X - M$, namely, the current account equals the difference between domestic saving $(S = Y - C)$ and domestic investment.

deteriorate indefinitely. It ignores, however, that the exchange rate will move to adjust the current account to the level determined by U.S. spending patterns. Thus if U.S. competitiveness declined for some reason—for example, if Americans developed a taste for foreign automobiles—the exchange rate would depreciate until the current account moved back to its original level. Perhaps some selective policy measures could restore the competitiveness of U.S. automobiles, but such measures would have costs for U.S. taxpayers and consumers. Thus two types of adjustment need to be compared: (1) an exchange rate change that alters the relative position of all U.S. firms competing in international trade and then induces resource flows at the margin across a wide number of sectors, and (2) selective policies in which the government induces resource flows with quotas, subsidies, tariffs, and so on. Both types are costly. An exchange rate devaluation normally results in a decline in the terms of trade.[16] Selective measures result in distortions of resource allocation imposed by taxes, tariffs, quotas, loan guarantees, and the like.[17] *Thus the key issue is whether or not a selective government intervention could improve on the adjustment costs associated with a change in exchange rates.* Can centralized government allocation of resources be more efficient than the decentralized decisions of the market?

Proponents of selective industrial policies for the United States often deny that they would have the government "pick winners and losers." But picking winners and losers apparently has a different meaning for different people: to some it means the government alone determines which firms will succeed or fail. In this extreme form, to be sure, few industrial policies pick winners. Yet the aim of all selective policies is to allocate resources to various industries in ways different from those of the market. In this sense, inevitably some industries will be favored and, implicitly, others will not. Some proposals seek to avoid providing explicit criteria by which resources would be allocated and instead designate a committee or a board and give it the responsibility for making such choices. But this simply postpones the inevitable question that board members would have to answer explicitly or implicitly—to avoid government assistance on a pork barrel basis, other economic criteria

16. This does not necessarily hold in theory, but tends to be true for large industrial countries such as the United States.
17. Trade protection hurts consumers; selective investment subsidies are costly to taxpayers; and loan guarantees impose costs on borrowers competing for funds.

would be necessary. What would these criteria be? Krugman notes that four such criteria are frequently mentioned: (1) key or "linkage" industries, (2) industries with high value added per worker, (3) future international competitiveness, and (4) industries favored by foreign industrial policies.[18] Below I consider whether these criteria are likely to allocate resources efficiently.

"LINKAGE" INDUSTRIES. Some point to "forward linkages" from key inputs such as steel, textiles, semiconductors, and machine tools and suggest that domestic production of these products is essential for industries such as automobiles, apparel, and machinery. Others point to "backward linkages" from complex products such as automobiles and aircraft and suggest that domestic production of these final goods is essential for the suppliers of component materials.

But the economy is an interdependent system of industries. Almost all industries are interconnected; therefore this criterion does little to narrow the selection process. It is widely acknowledged that private markets may fail when there are spillovers (or externalities), such as pollution, which are not accounted for in private incentives. Simply because one sector supplies inputs to another, however, does not imply the presence of such spillovers. Since a supplying industry can capture in its profits the benefits of such production, there is no reason to expect underinvestment in a sector that produces inputs.

Protecting input industries may, in fact, be particularly costly. If protection raises input costs, it will exert pervasive damage on the international competitiveness of finished products. For example, high prices for steel and machine tools will hurt numerous industries such as metal products, machinery, aircraft, shipbuilding, and automobiles. To survive in global competition, it is crucial that makers of complex products obtain their inputs from the cheapest sources. On the other hand, protecting finished products will not prevent producers from using offshore sources. Indeed, recognition of this fact lies behind proposals for domestic content legislation.

HIGH VALUE ADDED PER WORKER. Economies with high living standards have high levels of value added per worker. They also tend to have higher proportions of their resources in industries in which value added per worker is relatively high. Accordingly, some see the contraction of

18. Paul R. Krugman, "Targeted Industrial Policies: Theory and Evidence," in *Industrial Change and Public Policy*, a symposium sponsored by the Federal Reserve Bank of Kansas City (FRB of Kansas City, 1983), pp. 125–26.

such industries as a threat to living standards and advocate selective industrial policies to maintain and expand employment in industries with high value added. According to Magaziner and Reich, "Our country's real income can rise only if . . . its labor and capital increasingly flow toward businesses that add greater value per employee."[19] It is erroneous to conclude that, because affluent economies have relatively large industries with high average value added per worker, expanding these industries will raise living standards and shrinking them will lower living standards. Nations are affluent because they have high per capita levels of factor endowments, such as physical and human capital and natural resources. Given these factor endowments, nations that are relatively wealthy will tend to have larger proportions of their output in industries with high value added per worker. Consider an extreme case: a country with no capital or land will naturally produce only labor-intensive products. By comparison, a country with capital will tend to have a relatively larger capital-intensive sector. But it need not always be the case that expanding the sector with highest value added per worker makes the greatest contribution *at the margin* to living standards.

Assuming that an expansion of industries with high value added per worker will raise living standards confuses average and marginal returns. Efficiency requires that resources be allocated so that their marginal product in all activities is equalized. Just because the average output per worker is higher in one industry does not imply that allocating more workers to that industry will raise the value of national product. If this were true, a country could simply move all workers into the sector with the highest average output per worker.[20] But this would not be desirable for several reasons. First, if the additional workers lack sufficient plant, equipment, land, and other inputs, average product per worker will decline. Second, even if they are equipped with additional factors of production, the prices of that sector's output and thus value added per worker will fall because the market will be flooded with such products. Market forces tend to allocate resources where their marginal returns are the highest. It is unlikely that a committee using average criteria could allocate resources more efficiently.

Value added per worker can be high for several reasons. In a

19. Magaziner and Reich, *Minding America's Business,* p. 4.

20. As Krugman points out, since the capital stock is limited, such a reallocation would initially create high unemployment. See his "Targeted Industrial Policy," pp. 127–28.

competitive economy, on the one hand, profits and interest per worker could be high because each worker operates with large amounts of physical capital or natural resources. On the other hand, wages per worker could be high because workers are highly skilled or highly educated. In a noncompetitive economy, high value added per worker could also reflect monopoly profits or the influence of strong unions. Yet these differences are overlooked if a nation supports all industries with high value added per worker. Where this high value added per worker reflects monopoly, national welfare may improve by finding cheaper substitutes. Eliminating monopoly power might well decrease value added per worker in previously monopolized industries. However, the benefits to consumers in the rest of the economy from acquiring the product of that industry more cheaply would outweigh the losses to the industry's producers. Granting trade protection to a sector with monopolies in the name of keeping living standards high entails particularly convoluted logic. Since wages in industries in which output is concentrated in a few firms are frequently far higher than average wages in the economy, such actions are highly inequitable; they implicitly tax consumers with average income levels in order to support the earnings of a few prosperous producers.

Despite its inherent analytical deficiencies, from a political point of view this criterion has broad appeal. Both "smokestack" and high-technology industries tend to have high value added per worker. Thus using high value added per worker as a selection criterion would enable an industrial policy to support both types of industry. However, in the case of the smokestack industries such as automobiles and steel, high value added per worker tends to reflect a high intensity of physical capital and high wages; in the case of high-technology industries, high value added reflects workers' skills and amount of education. The criterion of high value added per worker is also a poor one in predicting U.S. international competitiveness, for both U.S. manufactured exports and imports tend to have high average value added per worker. In the case of imports, however, the criterion reflects high physical capital-intensity; in the case of exports, intensity in human capital.

INTERNATIONAL COMPETITIVENESS. Offensive industrial policies seek to accelerate change. Advocates of this acceleration see the U.S. industrial malaise as a failure to move rapidly enough out of old industries and into new ones. They recommend that old industries should be restructured and new industries promoted, but assistance should only be granted to internationally competitive production activities. As Lester Thurow has argued, "The only legitimate goal is the creation of a world-class industry."[21] But how, operationally, does one recognize a world-class competitor? What are the specific criteria that would guide policy selection? Three measures are possible: the ability to increase shares in world markets, to achieve a positive balance of trade, and to operate profitably in the future without government assistance. But, as I argue below, none of these is likely to be satisfactory.

The share in world export markets is commonly used as an indicator of international competitiveness. However, some problems are associated with this measure. It might be far better to have a declining share of a growing market than a growing or large share of a declining market. An industry could be highly profitable, expanding rapidly, and sustaining a positive balance of trade and yet be losing shares in world markets. Imagine, for example, that the Bell Telephone Company invents the semiconductor. In the short run, since it has a monopoly regarding this product, its share in world markets is 100 percent. With time the market expands, and Bell is engaged in a highly profitable activity. Soon, however, other companies, some foreign, enter the market; the foreign companies make sales in the United States. As a result, Bell's share of the semiconductor market declines; its share of the domestic market will also decline. Provided that the market as a whole is expanding rapidly, this is not a reason to abandon production of semiconductors. Conversely, the producer of an obsolete product—say, anvils—might find its share of the world markets moving toward 100 percent, and yet such activity might be highly unprofitable. The market share measure, therefore, is inherently flawed.

Simply because an industry has a positive trade balance does not imply that spending society's next dollar on that industry is more beneficial to the trade balance or to total economic efficiency than spending it on an industry with a trade deficit. On the margin, it might be better to reduce comparative disadvantage than to promote comparative advantage. But a priori there is no way to tell. An industrial policy that sought to assist only those who could achieve a positive trade balance in the long run would direct assistance away from firms in import-competing industries. By contrast, a devaluation of the currency would aid all firms competing in international trade.

21. Thurow, "The Case for Industrial Policies," p. 13.

As Krugman points out, even if the government has chosen to assist an industry in which comparative advantage lies, it is still hard to prove that such a policy is efficient.[22] Efficiency entails not just specializing in industries that have a comparative advantage, but doing so at the right time. For example, the United States may be able to export nuclear fusion plants, but to speed up their development might waste resources as long as cheaper energy sources are available.

There are other practical problems associated with choosing industries that could achieve trade surpluses. What is the appropriate definition of the industry? Assume that a number of automobile companies find that their operations producing parts for small sports cars are experiencing competition from imports and request assistance. Should they be required to achieve an export surplus in, for example, sports car parts, car parts, sports cars, small cars, or cars in general? Even if such classification problems are solved, the more difficult task is to predict the future trade balance. An idea of the difficulty involved is gained by examining the state-of-the-art studies that have sought to explain past net trade balances. An analyst is likely to explain the past more successfully than to predict the future. Typically, such studies account for only about 20 percent of the total trade balance variance.[23] While variables such as worker skills and capital-labor ratios are significant in determining industry trade balances, a variety of permanent and transitory factors exist that are less easily taken into account. Accordingly, the criterion of future trade balances is unlikely to be operational.

The third possible criterion is to support only those industries that could eventually function without government support—that is, those capable of making a profit in the long run. This, of course, is the well-known argument for protection of infant industries. But future profitability is not sufficient to justify such protection. Future profits must be sufficiently large to outweigh the current social costs of protection. If an industry offers future profits, however, why are private entrepreneurs not willing to invest in it? Ultimately the infant industry argument implies a failure in the capital markets. One reason the market might fail is that the government forecasts such profits more accurately than the private sector. This is unlikely to be the case in practice. Even if the government

22. Krugman, "Targeted Industrial Policies," pp. 134–53.

23. Robert M. Stern and Keith E. Maskus, "Determinants of the Structure of U.S. Foreign Trade, 1958–76," *Journal of International Economics,* vol. 11 (May 1981), pp. 207–24.

has superior information, it need not undertake the investment itself. The government could simply release its information to the public and allow private markets to incorporate it in their investment decisions. In less-developed nations the relatively underdeveloped state of capital markets may justify support of infant industries, but the United States probably has the most sophisticated capital markets in the world. It is hard to believe that they would ignore clearly profitable investment opportunities. Although the criterion of allocating resources to profitable activities is therefore an efficient one, it is not clear why a selective industrial policy is required. The profits should be sufficient incentive.

MATCHING FOREIGN SUBSIDIES. "Targeting" industries is a common foreign practice. Accordingly, it is argued, the United States should match at home the assistance provided by foreign nations to their industries. This approach is advocated for two distinct reasons. The first is fairness; the second is national economic welfare. Some argue that international trade competition must occur on a "level playing field." Like domestic competition, it should entail competition between firms operating under similar rules of the game. Differences in the behavior of firms, rather than government support or other features of their environment such as tax laws or wage rates, should determine success or failure. Thus, the argument goes, it is only fair for the U.S. government to ensure that American firms do not lose sales to foreigners on the basis of their superior government support.

Yet in a pluralistic world, international trade is never fair in this way. Indeed, as economic theories tell us, trade occurs precisely because national environments provide different production conditions. Among differences commonly acknowledged are climate, resource endowments, factor endowments, preferences, and income levels. Yet other differences are the result of deliberate social choices. Competitive pressures experienced by U.S. firms because of foreign subsidies are not in principle different from pressures resulting from better educational systems, greater tolerance of pollution, more laxity in regulation, or even lower wages.

The social choices a nation makes will also affect international competitiveness. This form of "unfairness" is part of the price of global trade in a pluralistic world. After all, taking foreign policies as given, the benefits of international specialization and comparative advantage are still available to the nation.

The mere presence of a foreign subsidy need not put U.S. firms at a competitive disadvantage. If the government provided an equal subsidy to all forms of production, overall resource allocation would remain unaffected. Similarly, a benefit provided to all firms, such as a value added tax levied only on domestic sales, could leave resource allocation unaltered. Since such taxes may leave comparative advantage unchanged, they do not provide foreigners with an unfair advantage.[24] Indeed, in principle, with some countries targeting high-technology firms and others targeting low-technology, trade flows and the competitive advantage of U.S. firms could be unaffected.

Would matching foreign subsidies improve U.S. welfare? Taking foreign subsidies as given, targeting the same industries could have adverse effects on U.S. national welfare if the United States produced goods at home that could be purchased more cheaply abroad. Because foreign governments typically grant assistance to their industries competing with declining U.S. industries, matching would lead the United States to place more resources into its industries that should be avoided. There are some situations in which government intervention might improve welfare, but mindlessly matching foreign targeting is not one of them. Industrial policy would of course require additional criteria if the United States ventured to deviate from foreign patterns of subsidy.

Implementation of Selective Industrial Policies

Each criterion considered in the preceding section is inherently flawed and likely to be inefficient. Indeed, this exercise underscores the problems associated with allocating resources on the basis of the characteristics of industry. Efficiency requires decisionmaking at the margin and a continuous reevaluation of the areas in which resources are most needed. There is no such thing as an absolute need. Instead there is need for continuous trade-offs. The market system can accomplish this through millions of independent consumers guiding marginal resource allocation decisions with their dollar votes. No central committee is likely to do better. Rather than assuming that some simple rules could select the truly deserving industries, a superior approach is to leave resource allocation to market forces unless there is a clear case of market failure.

24. For a discussion of this point see John Mutti, *Taxes, Subsidies, and Competitiveness Internationally* (Washington, D.C.: National Planning Association, 1982).

The search for criteria to define a basic or essential industry usually reflects a desire to find a reason for supporting an industry that is no longer required. If an industry producing commercial goods needs government support in order to function, in fact, that signals it is no longer basic. As Herbert Stein puts it: "The whole notion that some industries are basic is hollow. There are some basic needs—food, clothing, perhaps even some durable goods. But these and most other things can be bought for money. We should identify as basic industries only the ones that most efficiently earn for us the money to buy what we want. If the most efficient way for the U.S. to get steel is to produce tapes of *Dallas* and sell them to the Japanese, then producing tapes of *Dallas* is our basic industry."[25]

The focus on certain industries and modes of production marks nations as victims of their time. In the transition from an agricultural to an industrial economy, there arose in eighteenth-century France a group of people known as the physiocrats who believed that agricultural production was the source of all wealth. Today this notion seems rather quaint. In the current transition to an economy centered on technology and services, a similar widely held view holds that the production of goods from heavy industry is the source of wealth. In the twenty-second century such views will undoubtedly seem equally quaint. Nonetheless, moving from an agricultural to an industrial society left the world with an agricultural system shackled with government trade barriers. Similarly, it would be most unfortunate if the move from a society centered around heavy industry to one centered around knowledge-based manufacturing of services left the world with a global industrial policy system in which nations are hampered by similar fetters.

Implementation of a Selective Industrial Policy

Advocates of a selective industrial policy for the United States believe that a government development bank is needed. They argue that a confused marketplace tends toward myopia and an overvaluation of short-run profits. A government development bank would provide patient capital for long-term investments and eliminate the market's long-term capital deficiency. Yet, as I indicated above, there is no convincing evidence of such lacunae in U.S. financial markets.

25. "Don't Fall for Industrial Policy," *Fortune* (November 14, 1983), pp. 64–78.

Another alleged deficiency in the U.S. capital market is said to be the regulatory constraints that prevent U.S. banks from taking long-term equity positions in corporations. As Lester Thurow sees it, U.S. capital markets are deficient because they lack the investment banks that are found abroad. Indeed, regulators in the United States have been particularly wary of the potential abuses when deposit-receiving institutions take equity positions and have tried to prevent the development of such institutions. However, other financial institutions have developed in the United States that achieve very much the same objectives as investment banks do abroad—in particular, the horizontal conglomerates.[26]

In the United States there are many ways in which new businesses can obtain venture capital and old firms can move into new ventures. If the regulations that prevent investment banks are viewed as a major obstacle, the appropriate policy is to change the regulations rather than to establish a new government institution. Indeed, recent changes in regulations concerning export-trading companies are an example of such a modification.

It is also alleged that the U.S. capital market is unable to raise funds for large projects. But, in fact, there are few projects so large that they cannot be handled by that market. U.S. automobile companies, for example, have been able to finance a $40 billion investment over a five-year period. Generally the constraint on financing stems from questions about profitability rather than about the amount of funding required. In cases in which clear social purpose exists—for example, the space program, the development of synthetic fuels, or the Alaskan pipeline—such activities can be supported by the government as they have been in the past on a case-by-case basis.

Providing low-interest loans need not necessarily add to net investment but might simply subsidize already planned investments. If provided unconditionally, such loans could boost the wages of strong unions rather than investment in new plant and equipment. To avoid this, proponents of a new banking institution argue that such loans should be made subject to a set of conditions—the industry must invest in new plants, labor and management must accept lower wages, and so on. Could a selected panel of loan officers know what is required to make an industry competitive? If only a small loan is required to make the industry

26. For a theoretical justification for the existence of conglomerates, see Oliver E. Williamson, "The Modern Corporation: Origins, Evolution, Attributes," *Journal of Economic Literature*, vol. 19 (December 1981), pp. 1537–70.

profitable and internationally competitive, the question remains, Why is the private sector unaware of this profitable opportunity? If large amounts of money are required, the question is then, Why should the public sector be taking the risk?

The U.S. steel industry is often suggested as an ideal recipient of funds from the proposed bank. However, as the proponents of protectionism have seen, those firms benefiting from protection do not necessarily reinvest such benefits in their own industry. In particular, the 1982 purchase of the Marathon Oil Company by the U.S. Steel Corporation is frequently cited as an example. Yet, as such examples indicate, the managers themselves doubt the future long-run viability of the industry. When managers, familiar with the prospects of an industry, decide that it would be better to pay out higher dividends or to diversify away from a particular industry, they are not necessarily being shortsighted. They may indeed have the long run in mind and recognize the difficulties of restoring competitiveness. Thus the influence of the proposed bank may force managers to overlook the warning signals of a declining industry and lead them to pursue inappropriate action.

If loans by this bank result in more investment, they will not necessarily increase employment. Capital subsidies increase employment only if they result in an increase in demand, which more than offsets the labor displaced by the higher level of mechanization.[27] Thus such policies might not only entail a waste of social resources; if their objective is to provide jobs, they might actually be counterproductive!

At the technological frontier there is no compelling reason to believe that government officials are better able than the private sector to predict technological breakthroughs. Government support for basic and generic R&D may be needed (see the next chapter), but there is no convincing case to be made for a government corporation that takes equity positions in the commercialization of high-technology activities. As Nelson notes, governments have not had successful track records in such ventures.[28] Those proposing such plans imply that the capital market is misinformed about the prospects of such investments. Yet investing in new product

27. In his study of the U.S. textiles industry, Peter Isard found that employment per unit of output with new plant and equipment requires between 35 and 49 percent of the unit-labor requirement of marginally profitable equipment. By encouraging more capital-intensive methods, protection of textiles actually reduced employment. See Peter Isard, "Employment Impacts of Textile Imports and Investment: A Vintage-Capital Model," *American Economic Review,* vol. 63, no. 3 (June 1973), pp. 402–16.

28. Richard R. Nelson and Richard N. Langlois, "Industrial Innovation Policy: Lessons from American History," *Science,* vol. 219 (February 18, 1983), pp. 814–18.

development is an extremely risky undertaking. For the few plans that succeed, there will be many that fail. The centralized allocation of risk capital is likely to be biased against the mavericks. Thus a diversified strategy that depends upon incentives in the private capital markets may be more successful than one placing faith in the judgment of a central committee.

Industry as a Policy Unit?

The philosophy behind selective industrial policies reflects a particular world view: it assumes that clearly defined homogeneous products are made in nationally based industries with distinct characteristics and boundaries. The world market in each product goes to the nation that excels in whatever product feature counts the most in a specific situation—price, quality, technology, and so on.

Countries eventually specialize completely in industries in which they lead and lose completely those in which they lag. Since industries are distinctive, they are natural units for policy. To obtain a particular objective, governments should support industries with desirable characteristics; to raise living standards, promote those with high value added per worker; to meet national defense needs, preserve those that make key defense inputs; to revitalize regions, subsidize industries located there; and to be internationally competitive, choose industries in which comparative advantage lies.

But this view of the world is seriously inaccurate. The approaches specified by industrial policies are not well designed for the complexities of reality in which products are differentiated; production is globally integrated; industries encompass wide arrays of skills, processes, products, and plant locations; and competition is multidimensional, encompassing many features of products, such as price, quality, image, and servicing. In today's world, since industrial specialization is rare, intraindustry trade is the norm and thus choices are not about discrete issues such as selecting industries or losing them, but about where, at the margin, additional new resources should be allocated.[29] These are

29. Intraindustry trade takes several forms. First, trade in products at different stages of completion occurs because production processes are internationally specialized. Vertically integrated companies may make parts in the United States, send them abroad for offshore assembly in labor-intensive plants, and then reimport them for final distribution as finished products at home. Second, intraindustry trade in differentiated

choices that a centralized decisionmaker is ill-suited to make. The belief that once an industry gets ahead of its international rivals its competitors can never catch up is wrong. Indeed, the convergence of other industrial countries to U.S. productivity levels is clear evidence that there are advantages in coming from behind.

In principle, it is appealing to force an industry to formulate its own revitalization plan, which the government would support with protection, loans, and other forms of assistance. But in practice, implementation of such programs is difficult and risky. What constitutes a quorum for such assistance? What if, as is likely, just part of the industry endorses the plan? On the one hand, provision of aid to the entire industry when only some are prepared to meet government preconditions runs into the "free rider" problem; on the other, providing government assistance to just a few specific projects or firms creates unfair competition for domestic firms.

One means by which an industrial policy would operate is a quota or tariff on imports. Yet this would create free riders. Trade protection raises domestic prices and thereby assists all producers of import substitutes. If compliance with an industry revitalization program is costly, there is an incentive for firms to avoid paying this cost while enjoying the benefits from protection. The government, therefore, must continuously monitor and enforce compliance. Thus industry-wide supervision and explicit cartelization often characterize revitalization programs abroad.[30]

---

products occurs because, in different countries, one can find groups of consumers with similar preferences and incomes so that, for example, both International Business Machines and Fujitsu can find buyers for their computers in the United States and in Japan. Third, trade can originate from the same industry, but in products that are essentially different. For example, apparel trade includes specialized designer clothes, typically made in developed countries, and standardized mass production garments increasingly made in developing countries. Fourth, intraindustry trade may even occur in identical products because users prefer diversified sources of supply, or because transportation costs give foreign suppliers an advantage in particular regional markets. For example, Canadians buy oil from the United States in the East while Americans buy oil from Canada in the West.

30. Arthur Denzau provides a fascinating account of Japanese attempts to reduce capacity in the textile industry. The government purchased surplus spinning looms, required registration of existing spindles and looms, and banned unregistered equipment. Yet "despite the elaborate registration system, new producers continually enter the industry to the extent that the number of small establishments actually increased, and the estimated number of illegal looms in production almost exactly cancelled the effective subsidies to reduce capacity." See Arthur T. Denzau, "Will an Industrial Policy Work for the United States?" (St. Louis: Washington University, Center for the Study of American Business, September 1983).

Policies governing industries invariably convey unintentional benefits for free riders and are thus inefficient for achieving specific social objectives. If there is some social policy objective not reflected in private incentives, it should be realized with policy tools that are the most direct means of obtaining such objectives. Thus if the goal is to reduce pollution, for example, all products can be banned whose production yields pollution. But this policy would be imprecise. It would not differentiate between products according to the degree of pollution. It would provide no incentive for producers to reduce pollution at the margin. A tax levied in proportion to the amount of pollution, however, could have the desired effects.

An example of the flaws in aggregating entire industries to achieve specific goals is demonstrated by the arrangement regarding international trade in textiles, known as the multifiber agreement.[31] This agreement is ostensibly to protect poor workers and small firms in clothing, yet it protects giant and highly competitive, high-technology companies that produce yarn and synthetic fibers in the same way it protects labor-intensive sweat shops simply because both make a product labeled textiles. Agricultural policies are a second example. To support the incomes of poor farmers, public policy supports farm prices. Yet this policy provides the greatest benefits to the farms and corporations that produce the most crops, and inadvertently benefits the wealthy. Making direct payments to poor farmers, however, is more efficient. It is inefficient to confer benefits on an entire industry because of a concern for a relatively small number of workers or areas. These should be assisted directly.

A third example is the protection of sectors to accomplish the distribution of income. It has become common to note the erosion of the relative number of high-paying industrial jobs. Indeed, some have argued that as a result America is losing its middle class. But assume for a moment this were true. What should the response be? Some advocate trade protection. But this inflicts costs on consumers and protects the jobs of many from both upper and lower classes. If the problem is really the distribution of income, the efficient solution will require taxes and subsidies to redistribute income, rather than trade protection.

A final example is the goal of national defense. Many suggest that the government should protect a particular industry because it has an important role in national defense. Although there are undoubtedly

31. General Agreement on Tariffs and Trade, *Basic Instruments and Selected Documents,* Twenty-first Supplement, 1973–74 (Geneva: GATT, 1975), pp. 3–19.

legitimate reasons for maintaining domestic production capacity of particular defense products, there is no need to protect an entire industry Financial support for a few specific plants or the holding of stockpiles of strategic commodities might well accomplish the national defense objec tive. Thus, for purposes such as increasing employment, redistributing income, developing regions, or maintaining the national defense, there are invariably more precise methods than industrial policies available to meet objectives.

Practical Problems

Several additional characteristics of the U.S. political system suggest caution in adopting selective industrial policies. The United States has deliberately created a system of checks and balances in which a wide variety of groups operating through diverse channels may affect out comes. This implies, inevitably, that U.S. policies which fail to reflect an overwhelming national consensus are contradictory, uncoordinated and the outcome of chance as much as of deliberate construction. In such a system, selectively promoting industries would create a chaotic situation. An unelected group would select the projects; Congress, often subject to groups that seek to prevent change, would appropriate the funds; and an impermanent bureaucracy, with a four-year time horizon would carry them out. If implemented by a Democratic administration such policies would probably be reversed if a Republican administration followed. And, inevitably, policy would become captive to legal proce dures in a system that has always mistrusted bureaucratic discretion.

Advocates of an offensive selective industrial policy for the United States argue that inadvertently the United States has become increas ingly protectionist. Blinded by an ideological commitment to free mar kets, policymakers have granted protection as an exceptional and temporary response to unusual circumstances. Firms given protection have not been required to restore their competitiveness, and inevitably such protection has become permanent. Thus the United States has stumbled into a form of "lemon socialism" with a growing number of losers permanently on the protectionist dole. A coherent industrial policy, these observers argue, will provide greater access to government assistance but toughen conditions on which it is granted. In particular, aid would require a plan designed by the industry for becoming a world class competitor. As Thurow sees it, plans would be jointly determined by the firms, unions, the industries, and the banks and its suppliers. "If no such plan could be developed or if the people in the industry were not willing to make the new investments, wage concessions, or whatever else was necessary to make the industry fully competitive, government would not be willing to extend any form of aid."[32]

Easier access to government aid and the provision of more resources to distressed firms could cost more than current policies do. The proposed policy entails a gamble—more protection now in the hope of less protection later. In the current U.S. policymaking environment, is this a bet that is likely to pay off? There are reasons for skepticism. If the strategy is to succeed, a clear and unequivocal consensus must exist that assistance is limited to firms and sectors that could eventually compete autonomously. Without this consensus, expanding the scope of assistance could backfire. The result would be more protection and less adjustment. Currently a broad array of interest groups has embraced the proposals for selective industrial policies; some supporters have goals that are considerably different from meeting the test of the international marketplace. Some proponents of defensive industrial policies argue that the United States should not accept the impact of trade passively. They seek an industrial policy to make trade more fair by matching foreign government subsidies. Until foreigners change their behavior these critics seek to retain such U.S. subsidies. They also argue that the United States has to maintain entire industries—for purposes of national defense, to provide employment, supply key inputs for other industries, and promote regional economies, jobs with high value added, even a diversified industrial base.[33] As long as goals such as these enjoy support from politically powerful interests, there are strong reasons to suspect that new industrial policies would not be limited to future international competitiveness. Moreover, current U.S. trade laws grant protection in numerous instances in which international competitiveness is not a prerequisite. Safeguard clauses assist industries suffering injury from foreign competition; quotas protect industries regardless of their behavior; and antidumping laws protect firms when foreign selling prices are judged too low. If the offensive strategy were strictly followed, these

32. Thurow, "The Case for Industrial Policies," p. 2.
33. See the Labor-Industry Coalition for International Trade, *International Trade, Industrial Policies, and the Future of American Industry* (Washington, D.C.: LICIT, April 1983).

provisions would need modification or repeal. It is inconceivable that industries enjoying benefits from these rules will accede to their removal. Inevitably, therefore, exceptions to this criterion for support will be made. Once this is done, however, the new protection will be a supplement to rather than a substitute for the old.

History suggests that skepticism is warranted when the goals of eventual free trade are met by plans to withdraw from the current international trading rules. The international textiles agreements are a case in point. The first article of the multifiber agreement provides for "progressive liberalization of world trade." Yet the successive arrangements, first signed in 1962 and still in effect more than twenty years later, have become increasingly restrictive in nature and comprehensive in scope.

As Charles Schultze points out, selective programs introduced with specific goals have generally had a poor record of achievement in the United States.[34] The model cities program, which was to concentrate large amounts of resources in a few key urban regions, was successively diluted until it provided thin, but widely dispersed, assistance to 150 cities. Likewise, the qualifications for the Economic Development Administration program, which aids depressed regions, were continuously broadened until about 80 percent of the counties in the United States qualified. Given the inherent difficulties of forecasting internationally competitive industries alluded to above, a broad array of U.S. industries would soon receive support if a selective industrial policy were put into effect.[35]

Finally, the widespread provision of government assistance will have unfortunate consequences for U.S. industrial structure and managerial and worker incentives. Worker-manager cooperation is obviously desirable, but labor-management coalitions at the industry level can centralize power and decisionmaking in existing firms and unions at the expense of

34. Charles L. Schultze, "Industrial Policy: A Dissent."
35. Indeed, Philip H. Trezise has analyzed the allocation of credit in Japan by the Japanese Development Bank. See "Industrial Policy Is Not the Major Reason for Japan's Success," pp. 13-18. In the first twenty years of its existence, three-quarters of its funds went to merchant shipping, electric utilities, and regional and urban development. The steel industry received less than 1.0 percent, $110 million of its financing. Since 1972, steel investment in new technologies, excluding energy, has averaged only $313 million a year. Thus, as Charles Schultze concludes, "In Japan as in any other democratic country, the public investment budget has been divvied up in response to diverse political pressures." See Schultze, "Industrial Policy: A Dissent," p. 7.

both potential new entrants and consumers. It is no accident that Japan addresses the problem of declining industries by explicitly forming crisis cartels. It is also no wonder that proposals for industrial policy often enjoy support from both business and organized labor. For such policies replace selection by the marketplace with selection by government and, naturally, the forces most skilled in influencing such decisions find these policies attractive.

Conclusions

In the absence of a shift in macroeconomic policies, selective industrial policies may change the composition of the trade balance and employment but are unlikely to affect their aggregate levels.

The debate about selective industrial policies is thus not about how to increase employment or improve the trade balance, but about how best to allocate resources. Proponents of selective industrial policies seek to alter the outcome resulting from market forces by developing an alternative notion of desirable industrial structure. Although some avoid providing precise criteria for allocating resources, others have suggested favoring linkage industries, those with high value added per worker, those favored by foreign targeting, and those able to become competitive in the future. These criteria are likely to be inefficient. Simply because an industry may become internationally competitive does not imply that the efficient way to achieve a given trade balance is to promote it. An industry may have high average value added per worker, but that does not imply that society's living standards will be raised if it expands. An industry may provide inputs for other sectors, but it does not necessarily follow that there are gains, not captured by producers in that industry, that justify additional social support.

For a number of reasons industries are unlikely to be appropriate units for government support: they are extremely diverse; support organized at the industry level invariably leads to cartelization; particular objectives—such as meeting national defense needs, redistributing incomes, and promoting regional development—can all be achieved by more precise policies; and a move toward greater government participation in resource allocation is unlikely to enhance efficiency given the U.S. political system and administrative traditions.

As I argue in the next chapter, many U.S. structural and trade policies could be improved, but the flaws in industry-wide targeting point to a superior approach—confine government intervention to clear cases of market failure in which policies have a reasonable chance of improving market performance; when intervening, ensure that policies are targeted to remedy market failure as precisely as possible.

CHAPTER SIX

Toward More Appropriate Structural Policies

IT is unfortunate that two options, that of continuing with current programs or of adopting a new set of selective industrial policies, have monopolized the debate about U.S. structural policies. Proponents of current programs show a healthy respect for the marketplace but tend to overlook areas in which government intervention in both the United States and other countries may be desirable, beneficial, and inevitable. Proponents of selective industrial policies, on the other hand, recognize the need for adjustment strategies and programs but exaggerate the potential for selective government intervention in the United States.

This chapter offers a number of suggestions for reforming U.S. policy, while reflecting some general presumptions: structural policies should supplement market forces; policymakers should not try to select the most viable industries or firms; industry-specific programs should be kept to a minimum; and structural policies that enhance adjustment generally should be emphasized.

The goal of industrial policymakers should be to create an environment conducive to allocating capital and labor to activities with permanent growth potential in all sectors of the economy. The government should focus on recognized cases of market failure and on improving performance in industries in which government intervention is already widespread. This chapter deals with trade policy, improvement of policy coordination and transparency, facilitating adjustment, and correcting general market failures.

Policies Governing International Trade

U.S. postwar trade policy has been the result of two distinct processes: international negotiations initiated, organized, and dominated by the

117

United States, which have served to lower global import restrictions and develop a set of trading rules compatible with liberalization; and restrictive acts that have sometimes been the price paid for achieving overall liberalization and have reflected the abilities of special interests to use the U.S. political system for their own ends.[1]

The overall thrust of U.S. trade policy has been toward establishing free trade.[2] The United States has played a pivotal role in the reduction of trade barriers in the global economy. American initiatives resulted in the formation of the General Agreement on Tariffs and Trade in 1948 (GATT), followed by tariff negotiating sessions in the subsequent decades. This U.S. drive toward open, competitive markets and nondiscrimination among trading partners has reflected the assumption, held by many in both political parties, that an open global trading system was in the nation's interest and that U.S. leadership could accomplish liberalization through international negotiations.[3]

Although the overall focus of U.S. policies was on liberalization, there was also a second, less important but apparently inconsistent and contradictory trend toward the growing exclusion of products from the liberalization process. As Vernon argues, the coexistence of these two opposing strands was the natural result of the changing U.S. position in the global economy and the U.S. system of government.[4] As foreign nations began to match U.S. production capabilities, American producers felt growing pressure from international competition. Reflecting these pressures, the U.S. industries seeking assistance have gradually moved up the technological spectrum—first agriculture, then textiles,

1. The two strands in U.S. trade policy are traced in Raymond Vernon, "International Trade Policy in the 1980s: Prospects and Problems," the Edmund James Lecture (University of Illinois at Urbana-Champaign, Department of Political Science, 1981).

2. For a convincing analysis of the strength of the forces of free trade see Robert A. Pastor, *Congress and the Politics of U.S. Foreign Economic Policy, 1929–1976* (Berkeley: University of California Press, 1980).

3. Postwar U.S. policy was in part a response to the disastrous consequences of the Smoot-Hawley Tariff Act of the 1930s; under this act U.S. tariff policy set off a global spiral of self-defeating "beggar-thy-neighbor" policies manifested in protectionist actions and competitive devaluations. However, subsequent U.S. trade policy was not simply the result of a lesson learned from this experience or an ideological commitment toward free trade; it was also a policy based on the international, political, and economic interests of the United States. In contrast to its foreign counterparts, U.S. industry thrived during the war, and in almost every manufacturing sector U.S. firms were global leaders and had little trouble competing in international markets.

4. Vernon, "International Trade Policy in the 1980s."

then steel and automobiles and, increasingly, high-technology products such as semiconductors.

Power to determine trade policy is widely diffused in the United States.[5] It is shared by the president, Congress, and a quasi-judicial body, the International Trade Commission. The First Article of the U.S. Constitution gives Congress the power to regulate commerce with foreign nations, and Congress jealously guards this power by limiting the president's ability to negotiate tariff reductions.[6] By successfully lobbying Congress, therefore, industries can receive protection. By successfully petitioning the International Trade Commission to prevent injury from imports, or unfair trade practices, firms, trade associations, unions, and groups of workers can induce presidential action that contradicts the overall thrust of his policies. Thus every administration since that of President Truman has deemed it necessary to make protectionist concessions—either to obtain congressional acceptance of bills permitting further liberalization or to resist protectionist pressures regarded as even less acceptable.[7] Over time, protection to individual groups has accompanied lower U.S. tariffs and growth in trade.

On balance, however, the overall outcome has been greater liberalization of the U.S. market. Although it allowed individual industries to obtain protection, the diffused nature of the U.S. system contributed to the overall free trade thrust. For major industries, the executive branch has been able to negotiate arrangements such as trigger prices for steel on a case-by-case basis to avoid measures imposed by Congress. Congress has been able to voice constituency concerns in a protectionist manner and to send signals to U.S. trading partners, secure in the knowledge that the president would veto such legislation. Another factor, as Vernon points out, is that foreign exporters and importers associated

5. Indeed, the dispersion of power in the U.S. system allows Congress and the president to avoid full responsibility for trade policy. See, for example, J. M. Finger, H. Keith Hall, and Douglas R. Nelson, "The Political Economy of Administered Protection," *American Economic Review*, vol. 72 (June 1982), pp. 452–66.

6. Until a 1983 Supreme Court decision, Congress could also override presidential refusal to sign congressional protectionist measures into law or his refusal to follow the advice of the International Trade Commission. See *Immigration and Naturalization Service* v. *Chadha*, 28 U.S.C. 1252 (1983).

7. Robert E. Baldwin, "Protectionist Pressures in the United States," in Ryan C. Amacher, Gottfried Haberler, and Thomas D. Willet, eds., *Challenges to a Liberal Economic Order* (Washington, D.C.: American Enterprise Institute for Public Policy Research, 1979), pp. 223–38.

with them have been able to use the U.S. system to counteract the power of firms seeking import protection.[8] And, as Destler has observed, the U.S. domestic system for managing trade policy has been able to deal with industries individually and thereby avert "log-rolling" by a broad anti-import coalition.[9]

There is now a possibility that the free trade direction of U.S. policy could be reversed. Protectionist pressures facing the Reagan administration have probably been greater than those facing any administration in the postwar period. Macroeconomic policies implemented between 1980 and 1983 strengthened the dollar and brought about an exceptionally large trade deficit at a time of high unemployment. Given these economic conditions, the internal procedures for mitigating the adverse effects of trade have become strained. Multilateral trade negotiations serve as a useful counter to domestic pleas for assistance from unfair trade practices and allow the president to keep the trade policy initiative. But the worldwide recessionary conditions in 1981 and 1982 have prevented the initiation of a new mulitilateral trade round.[10] Because the administration has reduced the scope of the trade adjustment assistance program, it has been without the option of using this program to defuse requests for aid—a tactic that was used successfully by both presidents Gerald Ford and Jimmy Carter, especially in election years.[11] Thus despite its ideological commitment to free trade, the Reagan administration has been forced to grant protection: it has raised duties on imported motorcycles and placed quotas and duties on imports of specialty steel in response to findings by the International Trade Commission. And, even without such findings, it has sanctioned a tightening of restrictions on textiles trade, reintroduced quotas on sugar, and obtained voluntary export quotas on Japanese automobiles.[12] In 1980, according to Balassa

8. Vernon, "International Trade Policy in the 1980s," p. 10.

9. I. M. Destler, "The American Trade Policymaking System: Is it Finally Unravelling?" (Washington, D.C.: Institute for International Economics, 1983).

10. Indeed, the ministerial meeting of the General Agreement on Tariffs and Trade in November 1982 was conspicuous for its limited achievements. See, for example, Robert E. Baldwin, "Trade Policies under the Reagan Administration," in Robert E. Baldwin, ed., *Recent Issues and Initiatives in U.S. Trade Policy,* National Bureau of Economic Research Conference Report (NBER, 1984), pp. 10–31.

11. See Gary Clyde Hufbauer and Howard Rosen, "Managing Comparative Disadvantage" (Washington, D.C.: Institute for International Economics, December 1983).

12. It should be noted that in 1981 the administration terminated the quotas on television sets and footwear. President Reagan also vetoed renewal of the manufacturing

and Balassa, 20.3 percent of U.S. consumption of manufactured goods was subject to nontariff import restrictions; by 1983, this had grown to 35 percent. The proportion was 28.4 percent for the European Common Market in the same year.[13] The postwar progress toward freer U.S. trade is now threatened. On the one hand stands an administration, ideologically committed to free trade, forced by pragmatic considerations to protect major industries with quotas. On the other hand, a host of alternative proposals—some nominally committed to rationalizing and to eventually reducing protection—would effectively ease the conditions under which particular industries are given protection.[14]

Despite the evidence in the chapters above that given appropriate policies the United States can compete, the problems of particular U.S. industries in an inhospitable environment could shift U.S. policies toward protectionism for three reasons: first, there is a widespread perception by U.S. firms that the international trading system is unfair; second, many believe that the amount of dislocation due to trade is unacceptable; and third, some observers think free trade threatens the national defense and foreign policy goals of the United States.[15] Thus U.S. trade policy is subject to three key questions: How should U.S. policy respond to "unfair" foreign government policies that distort

clause that requires books and periodicals written in English by Americans or foreigners domiciled in the United States to be printed and bound in the United States if they are to enjoy complete copyright protection. Congress responded with an override. See Raymond J. Ahearn and Alfred Reifman, "Trade Policymaking in the Congress," in Baldwin, ed., *Recent Issues and Initiatives in U.S. Trade Policy,* pp. 49–50.

13. Bela Balassa and Carol Balassa, "Industrial Protection in the Developed Countries" (Johns Hopkins University, March 1984).

14. Besides proposals for an industrial policy there have been serious legislative proposals for an aggressive policy of reciprocity and for local content requirements. See William R. Cline, " 'Reciprocity': A New Approach to World Trade Policy" (Washington, D.C.: Institute for International Economics, September 1982); Leonard Weiss, "Managing Trade Relations in the 1980's: Issues Involved in the GATT Ministerial Meeting—1982," paper of the research study panel (Washington, D.C.: The American Society of International Law, 1982); and Dick K. Nanto, "Automobile Domestic Content Requirements," Issue Brief IB82056 (Congressional Research Service, Library of Congress, November 1983).

15. It has long been recognized in the economic literature that in a number of instances free trade may not be optimal—for example, if the nation has some monopoly power it can use an optimal tariff (unfair trade); if private costs do not reflect social costs (externalities associated with dislocation); and if trade interferes with meeting the needs of national defense. These cases of market failure suggest the need for trade policies of the types discussed below.

goods, services, and investment flows? How can U.S. policy promote
efficient domestic adjustment to changes in international specialization?
What forms of trade intervention are appropriate for foreign policy and
national defense purposes? Below I address each of these questions in
turn.

Unfair Trade

It has been psychologically difficult for Americans to adjust to the
new international environment in which foreign production capabilities
are close to that of the United States and in which foreign governments
play a more active role in the economy than the U.S. government does.
Some seek to preserve and restore U.S. dominance by restricting the
international transmission of new technologies and retreating behind
trade barriers. But given the state of global communications, it is
impractical and inefficient to hinder technological diffusion. Legal strictures will not prevent the transfer of know-how, but they may prevent
U.S. firms from realizing the full benefits of their innovations by licensing
foreign production when it is profitable. Others implore the U.S. government to maintain the American lead in all products. Yet this strategy
could entail a wasteful U.S. duplication of foreign efforts.

The relative position of the United States after World War II was
bound to erode, but this relative decline did not make Americans worse
off. In fact, the postwar period has been one of the most prosperous in
the nation's history. Foreign successes, some of which may indeed be
due to foreign industrial policies, do not necessarily imply U.S. failure.
The frontiers of knowledge can be simultaneously expanded by a process
in which many firms and products can survive. Foreign efforts and
innovations should be applauded rather than discouraged, for the United
States can become the beneficiary of "reverse technology transfers."

Nonetheless, the world of trade appears unfair to U.S. firms. Firms
in other countries receive more government assistance than those in the
United States. However, efforts by the United States to emulate other
countries would probably result in no net gain and conceivably would
yield substantial losses for America and its trading partners. The most
straightforward policy guidelines for dealing with foreign industrial
policies are either (1) to ignore them and follow a policy of free trade,
that of laissez-faire, or (2) to match them. Serious problems are asso-

ciated with both approaches, however, and a more complex strategy is called for.

LAISSEZ-FAIRE. Some economic theorists assert that the laissez-faire approach is the correct one. Taking foreign behavior as given, U.S. trade protection hurts the United States. The unilateral reduction in U.S. protection would result in net benefits to the U.S. economy.[16] Baldwin has articulated the argument for the laissez-faire approach:

To the extent that there is a uniform element in various government subsidies, preferences, and regulations, movements in exchange rates and factor prices tend to offset any unfavorable balance of trade effects. Moreover, the differential effects among industries should be regarded in much the same way as the differential consequences of some underlying real factor affecting comparative advantage. The fact that a foreign government's subsidy policies place severe competitive pressures on certain U.S. industries, even after exchange rate changes resulting from the subsidies, is not in principle different from the fact that the existence of lower wages abroad puts severe competitive pressures on particular U.S. industries. If foreign governments want to use their own taxpayers' money to provide us with goods at lower prices than we can provide for ourselves, then we should welcome the addition to our living standards.[17]

But the laissez-faire approach ignores the strategic considerations that are inherent in trade policy.[18] It disregards the potential for deterrence inherent in protectionism. The threat of possible retaliation prevents other nations with monopoly power in trade from setting an amount of protection that maximizes their gains from trade. A strong commitment not to protect under any circumstances could leave the United States vulnerable to foreign monopoly power and unable to use reciprocal reductions in protectionism as a negotiating device. While foreign subsidies on exports to the United States may make Americans tempo-

16. Mutti analyzed the benefits of a unilateral tariff reduction in chemicals, iron and steel, machine tools, electrical machinery, and motor vehicles. See John Mutti, "Aspects of Unilateral Trade Policy and Factor Adjustment Costs," *Review of Economics and Statistics,* vol. 60 (February 1978), pp. 102–10.

17. Baldwin, "Protectionist Pressures in the United States," p. 236. For a discussion of this issue, see also Richard N. Cooper, "U.S. Policies and Practices on Subsidies in International Trade," in Stephen J. Warnecke, ed., *International Trade and Industrial Policies* (New York: Holmes and Meier, 1978), pp. 107–22. Cooper suggests "perhaps we should not worry so much about government subsidies to economic activity . . . provided [they] are introduced sufficiently gradually so that they do not impose acute adjustment costs on economic activities outside the country in question" (p. 120).

18. For a more complete discussion of strategic trade policy see J. David Richardson, "International Trade Policies in a World of Industrial Change," in *Industrial Change and Public Policy,* a symposium sponsored by the Federal Reserve Bank of Kansas City (FRB of Kansas City, 1983), pp. 267–313.

rarily better off, there is no assurance that such subsidies will be sustained should American firms be driven from the market. Furthermore, similar subsidies on goods that compete with American products in third markets may make Americans worse off.

MATCHING SUBSIDIES. The second approach, to match whatever subsidies foreigners provide their industries, would be impossible to administer and would simply compound the folly. The Commission of the European Communities, for example, would require governments to harmonize all assistance to and restraints on domestic economic activity so that the same incentives would apply to all producers. But at a global level such a system would be impossible to administer. It is unclear what "matching" requires if only some foreign competitors receive subsidies. If firms from Korea receive a 10 percent subsidy and those from Japan, 5 percent, how much assistance should their U.S. competitors be granted? Indeed, that is why countervailing duties on subsidized imports are more appropriate than efforts to match subsidies.

Would matching foreign subsidies improve U.S. welfare? Taking foreign subsidies as given, targeting the same industries could lower U.S. national welfare because the United States would have to produce goods at home that Americans could buy more cheaply abroad. Because foreign governments often grant assistance to declining industries (or, in the case of less-developed countries, to industries in which the U.S. comparative advantage is declining), matching would lead the United States to place more resources into the industries it should avoid. There are some situations in which government intervention might improve welfare, but matching foreign targeting is not one of them.

The mere presence of a foreign subsidy need not put U.S. firms at a competitive disadvantage. If the government provided an equal subsidy to all forms of production, overall resource allocation would remain unaffected. Similarly, a benefit provided to all firms such as a value added tax levied only on domestic sales could leave resource allocation unaltered. Since such taxes may leave comparative advantage unchanged, they do not provide foreigners with an unfair advantage.[19]

19. For a discussion see John H. Mutti, *Taxes, Subsidies, and Competitiveness Internationally* (Washington, D.C.: National Planning Association, 1982). Indeed, in the case of Zenith Radio Corp. *v.* United States (437 U.S. 443, June 1978) the U.S. Supreme Court found that the remission of indirect taxes by a foreign country does not constitute a subsidization of that country's exports.

In principle, with some countries targeting high-technology firms and others focusing on low-technology, trade flows and the competitive advantage of U.S. firms could be unaffected. The evidence from the 1970s does not suggest that foreign subsidies have made major distortions in U.S. trade patterns: U.S. comparative advantage reflects expected shifts in international development patterns.

If the United States does not follow straightforward guidelines, it still needs a strategy when responding to foreign practices. There is a third course: U.S. retaliation to foreign government policies should be confined to cases in which U.S. *national* economic welfare is clearly adversely affected and in which U.S. retaliation is likely to make the nation better off.

In general, the United States should permit trade even when foreign competitors receive direct government assistance. Some foreign government aid is not aimed directly at international trade, and in a pluralistic world, even though such aid may affect trade, this should be broadly tolerated—particularly when shifts in international competitiveness can occur at a reasonable pace and when, at a global level, excess capacity does not exist. Nor need the mere presence of foreign export subsidies imply that U.S. welfare will be damaged. This is especially true of foreign subsidies on U.S. imports. Some U.S. producers may experience competitive pressures, but U.S. consumers, and producers distributing imports and using them as inputs, usually have an offsetting gain. When do these policies threaten U.S. welfare? This could occur (1) if foreign subsidies lower the prices that U.S. exporters receive in foreign markets, (2) if subsidies are predatory, with foreigners driving out domestic producers in order to exert monopoly power, or (3) if the social costs of the dislocation of the producers outweigh the gains to U.S. consumers.

The United States could, where judgment suggests deterrence will be effective, match foreign export credits on products that are competitive with U.S. exports to foreign markets. Far more effective, however, would be an agreement with U.S. competitors to reduce and eventually eliminate government export financing. The United States should also encourage the application of international (GATT) laws against dumping in major U.S. export markets. America's duties on dumped products can be regarded as contributing to an international order in which such practices are prevented.

The United States should also use duties to offset foreign export subsidies on imports to the United States if there is a realistic and credible possibility of long-run predatory pricing practices.[20]

As this discussion suggests, the major legal provisions against unfair trade contained in U.S. law provide a reasonable basis for dealing with unfair trade practices, especially those in America. The provisions for countervailing duties and other remedies for dumping allow U.S. industry to offset such practices when an injury test is met. Although this does not exactly require proving that the costs of producer dislocation exceed consumer benefits, it is at least a step in that direction. Section 337 of the U.S. Tariff Act of 1930 makes unlawful unfair methods of competition that restrain or monopolize trade.

But the U.S. government should act in the spirit of its own laws. The appropriate remedy for unfair imports is a countervailing duty. As Robert Baldwin notes, however, rather than deal with the alleged subsidies on European steel exports to the United States with a duty that offsets the subsidies, the Reagan administration negotiated an agreement that quantitatively limited the majority of steel mill exports from the European Economic Community to the United States for a three-year period. He observes, "It is surprising that an administration committed to free but fair trade settled its major fair trade case with an arrangement that was not carefully designed to just offset the alleged subsidies and is regarded as the worst form of protection by free traders."[21]

REMOVING BARRIERS ABROAD. Because an open global trading system is in the interests of the United States, there should be major multilateral and bilateral initiatives to remove or weaken foreign barriers and open foreign markets. Economies of scale are important for firms producing high-technology products for which significant cost declines occur as production volumes rise. Accordingly, it is crucial that U.S. firms are not denied access to markets available to their competitors. Since the United States allows virtually open access to foreign high-technology firms and does not use infant industry tariffs, it should ensure that a similar access is provided for U.S. firms in markets of developed

20. The scope for such practices should not be exaggerated, particularly in an open world economy. Driving competitors out of the market by selling below cost only makes sense if future reentry can be prevented. Even if, for example, the domestic U.S. steel industry was dramatically reduced in size, the United States would not be vulnerable to predatory practices as long as it had numerous sources of foreign supply.

21. Baldwin, "Trade Policies under the Reagan Administration," p. 22.

countries. Open trade between the United States and Japan and reciprocal access by firms in one country to the other's market are particularly
important. U.S. and Japanese firms should be allowed to participate in
each other's industrial policy programs.

There are those who argue that before lowering trade barriers, one
may have to raise them. They advocate U.S. retaliatory protection used
against countries not granting market access that is "substantially
equivalent" to access in the United States. Such a course is risky,
disingenuous, and unnecessary. It is risky because it could escalate a
trade war. It represents a fundamental change in the historical practice
of most-favored-nation treatment, which has been so successful in
bringing down global trade barriers in the past. If the United States
granted discriminatory access to different trading partners, the practice
would highly politicize trading relationships. Such discrimination would
be costly to U.S. consumers and would introduce the possibility of
retaliation against U.S. exports abroad. It is disingenuous because often
proponents of such policies seek an excuse for protection—for example,
the loudest complaints about the closed nature of the Japanese market
often come from U.S. industries that have great trouble competing with
Japan in the United States and hence are unlikely to benefit from greater
access to the Japanese market. Finally, U.S. retaliatory protection
abroad is unnecessary because, without increasing U.S. trade protection, converting existing U.S. (and foreign) trade barriers into tariffs
would provide plenty of bargaining chips.[22] Moreover, as Deardorff and
Stern have pointed out, if the United States seeks to discourage other
governments from trade policies that are undesirable from America's
standpoint, there is no reason why U.S. trade policies should be used.
Political pressures of other sorts may be more effective and less costly
to the United States.[23]

Domestic Dislocation: Adjustment to Industrial Changes

The United States now has a relatively effective quasi-judicial procedure in which the International Trade Commission determines whether

22. Currently U.S. quotas give foreign exporters rents because quotas raise prices
in America. Tariffs would transfer these rents from the foreigners to the U.S. government.
23. Alan V. Deardorff and Robert M. Stern, "Current Issues in Trade Policy: An
Overview," Institute of Public Policy Studies Discussion Paper 185 (Ann Arbor,
Michigan: Institute for Policy Studies, April 1983), p. 25.

specific imports are a cause of serious injury to a domestic industry. Thus if the ITC makes a decision in favor of an industry, section 201 of the Trade Act of 1974 provides U.S. firms with a remedy, chosen by the president, which is best suited to "preventing serious injury or threat thereof to the industry . . . and to facilitate the orderly adjustment to new competitive conditions." The United States is less successful, however, in ensuring that industries adhere to their own legal processes and that protection facilitates adjustment.

As Hufbauer and Rosen note, there is a two-track system in U.S. trade policy: small industries usually work through legal channels; large industries do not.[24] Although large industries generally begin to address a problem through these same legal channels, they often circumvent them in search of special solutions. Indeed, major steps taken by the Reagan administration to ensure protection have circumvented the ITC process. The voluntary export restraints on Japanese automobiles were implemented despite the ITC rejection of the petition for import relief by the automobile industry; the bilateral export quotas negotiated with European steelmakers represented a rejection of remedies suggested by the ITC; and the reintroduction of sugar quotas and the tightening of the multifiber agreement in the textile industry did not involve the ITC at all.

The U.S. system needs to be strengthened so that only industries proving injury from trade obtain assistance and only tariffs are used in providing such assistance. This should be done with both "carrots" and "sticks." First, only industries supported by ITC decisions should be eligible for participation in the new trade adjustment assistance program (outlined in the next section). Second, whenever measures are taken by either the president or Congress that are not recommended by the ITC, a mandatory analysis should be required of the cost to consumers per job saved. Third, industries that are protected with tariffs in response to their requests for safeguard actions should receive more permissive treatment by antitrust authorities on requests for mergers, and so on.

TARIFFS. It is unfortunate that the Reagan administration has, in the cases of European steel and Japanese automobiles, shown a preference for explicit (or voluntary) quotas. A tariff, preset to decline over time, should be the only instrument allowed for safeguard actions. Tariffs

---

24. Hufbauer and Rosen, "Managing Comparative Disadvantage."

have numerous advantages over quotas.[25] One is that tariffs are transparent, in the sense that they make the extent of protection relatively clear.[26] The costs of quotas, on the other hand, are hidden. Another advantage of tariffs is that, although under conditions of perfect competition quotas and tariffs can have equivalent effects on domestic output and prices, if competition is less than perfect, quotas will tend to strengthen domestic monopolies. Since tariffs allow imports to enter freely at the tariff-inclusion price, raising domestic prices above such a price will mean that domestic producers will face increased imports. By contrast, with quotas in effect domestic producers need not fear a rise in imports.[27] Still another advantage of tariffs is that they reflect new changes in market conditions, but quotas do not. For example, if the foreign cost advantage over domestic producers rises from $10 to $1000 per item, quotas will be unresponsive. Finally, the revenue from tariffs accrues to the U.S. government; the increased profits earned from higher domestic prices under quotas, however, accrue to the foreign exporter.[28]

Consider, then, some of the likely effects of granting a quota to an industry with some monopoly power. First, the industry will tend to raise prices and lower output. Although its share of the domestic market might be increased, it could actually produce less than if free trade prevailed. Instead of raising employment and saving jobs, therefore, a quota could actually reduce employment! Second, since imports are effectively limited, the incentives to reduce costs and improve efficiency would be reduced. Third, such a policy could strengthen foreign competitors by affording them higher profit margins. In the case of so-called voluntary export restraints, foreign firms would be forced to collude to

25. The argument supporting tariffs does not imply they are usually the best instruments for policy. In theory tariffs are rarely the most efficient policy instrument because they distort *both* production and consumption decisions. Generally taxes or subsidies can be used to meet objectives more precisely. For a more complete exposition see Gerald M. Meier, *International Economics: The Theory of Policy* (New York: Oxford University Press, 1980), pp. 93–101.

26. Although they may be transparent, actual tariff levels may not accurately indicate levels of effective protection. For an explanation of the effective tariff see Meier, *International Economics,* pp. 118–20.

27. Indeed, if the quota were tied to market shares, a rise in domestic prices that restricted demand would also cut off imports.

28. This assumes, as is common in the case of U.S. import quotas, that the U.S. government does not sell rights to quotas to the highest bidder. In such cases the revenues accrue to the United States government.

allocate the volume they were permitted to export. By contrast, a tariff that produces the same initial reduction in imports would lead to lower prices for consumers (if domestic firms had monopoly power), more revenue for the U.S. government, less revenue for foreign producers, and greater incentives to improve efficiency and reduce costs.

It has become fashionable to argue that protection should depend on commitments by the domestic industry to take a variety of measures designed to restore competitiveness. Some would couple protection with government efforts to retire capacity and to restructure the industry itself. This approach assumes the government knows better than the industry what is required for such competitiveness. If an industry were provided by tariff protection with a respite that it knew to be temporary, there would be great incentive for the industry to take steps on its own to restore its competitiveness if it believed this could be done. It is essential, however, that the temporary protection provide the correct incentives.

The protection afforded by domestic content provisions is particularly unlikely to induce adjustment. In 1982, for example, the House of Representatives passed a bill requiring foreign producers selling more than 100,000 automobiles in the United States to use a certain percentage of American parts and labor. The bill has not yet become law. If passed, it would not only provide U.S. automobile manufacturers with a captive market but would create a market for firms supplying parts to the U.S. automobile companies. Numerous studies have indicated that poor management practices and poor labor-management relations have undermined the relative competitiveness of the U.S. automobile industry. American automobile workers also earn considerably greater premiums over average industrial wages than do their foreign counterparts.

This proposed legislation would undermine the pressures on U.S. automobile manufacturers to remedy their deficiencies in competitiveness; it would make it likely that if Japanese firms were to relocate in the United States, they would adopt U.S. management practices and pay U.S. wages. For they would be the captives of U.S. suppliers and unions, without the leverage of using foreign supplies to induce efficient performance.

The failure of U.S. protection to stimulate adjustment in the major sectors stems not from a failure of the government to obtain commitments from industry about revitalization, but from the counterproductive incentives created by the forms of protection chosen. Thus the United

States should replace its existing quotas, marketing arrangements, and so-called voluntary export restraints with tariffs preset to decline over time.[29]

TRADE ADJUSTMENT ASSISTANCE. Another way in which the United States has responded to changes in international specialization is to develop adjustment assistance to workers who suffer job loss because of changing conditions of trade. This assistance may have some justification if viewed in a political context as compensation for the removal of protection or as an inducement to accept safeguard protection with a compensating tariff.[30] In essence, there is room for a deal between society, which will benefit from lowering protection, and the producers, who will lose. But the existing trade adjustment assistance program thus far has failed to persuade producers to allow free trade. Many of the recipients have been from the steel and automobile industries, both of which currently have trade protection.

The trade adjustment assistance program is basically flawed because it distorts the incentives to adjust. U.S. trade adjustment assistance is provided primarily in the form of a supplement to unemployment compensation, but this compensates only workers who *fail* to adjust. Unemployment insurance is an all-or-nothing payment that is not modified to allow training or the acceptance of lower-paying jobs. Most program recipients eventually return to their original jobs.

Workers whose major asset lies in the specific human capital associated with a particular job cannot diversify the risk of having so much of their "wealth" invested in one activity. The removal of protection erodes the value of these workers' specific human capital. One form of compensation with less perverse incentive effects than present unemployment benefits might be a lump-sum payment. However, for workers who find alternative employment immediately at wages similar to their previous earnings this solution seems excessively generous. A superior compensation program would provide qualified workers with a payment

29. This suggestion was made by Hufbauer and Rosen. The government might face great uncertainty in obtaining the tariff equivalent of its quotas. One approach would be to first auction import licenses and then set tariffs initially at the import license price.

30. For a more complete discussion see C. Michael Aho and Thomas O. Bayard, "American Trade Adjustment Assistance after Five Years," *The World Economy,* vol. 3 (1980), pp. 359–76; and J. David Richardson, "Trade Adjustment Assistance under the United States Trade Act of 1974: An Analytical Examination and Worker Survey," in J. Bagwhati, ed., *Import Competition and Response* (University of Chicago Press for the National Bureau of Economic Research, 1982).

equal to a fixed percentage of the erosion in their earnings for a particular period of time. Thus, if the compensation ratio were 50 percent, a laid-off worker who had earned $20,000 a year and found a job with a salary of $10,000 might receive $5,000 for some subsequent time period once he found a new job. Trade adjustment compensation would be paid only after the worker found new employment.

Such a system would reduce the disincentive to work; it would provide the greatest compensation for those with the greatest loss of *specific* human capital as indicated by their relative salary loss. Rather than remain idle in the hope of reemployment with their old firms, workers could accept jobs paying relatively lower wages with the chance of building up seniority.[31]

The entitlement could be given to workers in an industry in which trade protection was being lowered and could be coupled with the provision of temporary protection if firms prove injury from imports as required for escape clause relief under section 332 of the Tariff Act of 1930. The program would not be made available to new workers who joined the industry after plans to remove trade barriers had been made public. The proportion of income to be replaced over time would also gradually decline. And the proportion of income replaced could also reflect the worker's age and experience. The United States could merge a program to provide adjustment assistance to workers displaced from the apparel and textile industries with a more liberal and ultimately free trade policy in these industries. Alternatively, it could use the prospect of lower trade barriers for textiles to obtain lower barriers for its exports abroad.

Such a program may sound expensive. But it would save on unemployment insurance by increasing work incentives. It would eventually mean savings for consumers, who might otherwise have to pay the higher prices resulting from protection. And over the long run foreign producers would derive the benefits of free entry to the U.S. market.

While they are relatively few in number, the problems confronting older displaced workers may be extremely severe. It would be far better for society to have a particular program to compensate such individuals

31. This form of payment, unlike a voucher system, would not provide "unfair" competition for other workers. And unlike vouchers, which compensate the firm rather than the worker, this payment plan would provide no incentive to fire such workers once the grant period ran its course.

for their loss than to attempt to prevent the effects of structural change on these persons by slowing the pace of technology or international specialization. A more general income-supplement program along these lines might be provided for elderly workers who are displaced, regardless of the reason for job loss. For younger workers general programs might seek to supplement retraining and relocation expenditures rather than supplement income.

Policies Related to U.S. Exports and National Defense

The United States places a large number of restrictive measures on U.S. producers who export. International trade is now used for a host of noneconomic measures, often with high costs and little effect.[32] The recognition that the United States has had major problems recently concerning its international competitiveness does not appear to have reduced the use of trade for political purposes, nor has policy reflected the ability of other industrial nations to supply substitutes for U.S. products. If anything, in recent years inhibitions on U.S. exporters have increased. Unilateral policies have been taken such as enforcement of the Foreign Corrupt Practices Act and restrictions on exports to Poland and on high-technology exports to the Soviet Union and Soviet bloc countries. There are new proposals to broaden these restrictions. In instances in which other developed countries make similar products, embargoes or controls should be used only if U.S. allies apply similar pressures. The regulations that hinder U.S. export performance should be reviewed in terms of the new international realities. Unilateral policies typically have adverse consequences for U.S. competitiveness and fail to achieve their political and security purposes.

The military sector is another area in which U.S. trade policy could be improved. Almost every U.S. industry that seeks trade protection argues that its output is essential for national defense.[33] Indeed, if certain

---

32. Gary Hufbauer and Jeffrey J. Schott, "Economic Sanctions in Support of Foreign Policy Goals" (Washington, D.C.: Institute for International Economics, 1983).

33. Basiuk sees ominous trends in the impact of eroding U.S. international competitiveness on national defense. Yet he concludes, after examining the effects of foreign competition on three U.S. industries, "The computer sector has not yet been affected at all. Even without the impact of foreign competition, the machine tools industry had very limited surge capacity. In consumer electronics and semiconductors, the losses in productive facilities are not very damaging." See Victor Basiuk, "Security Recedes," *Foreign Policy*, no. 53 (Winter 1983–84), pp. 49–73.

plants or firms have to be based domestically for U.S. military needs, they should be supported. But such support should not be provided indiscriminately through trade protection. Instead, all U.S. military needs should be met explicitly through the defense budget. U.S. national defense planners should be given an overall budget to spend on the best defense they can buy. Let them trade off their spending on strategic plants, supercomputers, and stockpiles against spending on soldiers and arms. If subject to an overall budget constraint, these planners would be unlikely to subsidize entire industries when the true military needs required less than the entire output. For example, although the steel industry is frequently mentioned as crucial for national defense, according to 1983 estimates, national defense accounted for about 7 percent of total U.S. steel consumption.[34]

Policy Transparency: Lack of Clarity and Adequate Data

A private market will not automatically generate the information necessary for public policy. Compiling social statistics is thus the appropriate responsibility of government, especially in a decentralized system with numerous decisionmakers and policymaking centers. But the current information on which U.S. structural policies are based is inadequate. Individual agencies provide reports about activities within their domain, but because there is no comprehensive inventory of *all* government policies or a detailed analysis of their net effects, it is impossible to evaluate the total influence of policy. The government provides industrial assistance through many different agencies and programs with limited notions of social costs and benefits. Vastly different sums of money are allocated from the public purse and the consumer's pocket to save specific jobs. Policies in different parts of the government work at cross purposes. And policies that are poorly designed, such as the current depreciation allowance schedules, inadvertently distort allocation across sectors.

These problems are not unique to the United States. Inadequate information and a lack of policy transparency, or lack of clarity,

34. Even after a massive defense buildup, by 1987 national defense will account for only 7.6 percent of iron and steel forging consumption and 5.2 percent of iron and steel foundry consumption. See U.S. Department of Commerce, Bureau of Industrial Economics, *1983 U.S. Industrial Outlook* (January 1983), p. xlii.

characterize the policies of many nations.[35] Since 1973, indeed, government involvement in all industrial economies has grown. Subsidies to depressed regions, funds to support R&D and increase employment, selective procurement, and subsidies for nationalized industries are all common. Other policies have been specifically directed toward influencing trade and have increasingly taken nontariff forms such as quotas, orderly marketing arrangements, and voluntary export restraints. Measures such as selective government procurement, quality and safety standards, and local content provisions discriminate against foreign firms. Exports have been promoted through credit subsidies.

The opaque nature of many of these new policies creates numerous problems. Tariffs are quantitative measures that are typically implemented on the basis of legislation. The new forms of protection in other countries are hard to measure and are carried out by executive bodies. Consequently, they are particularly difficult to confront. There is the danger of exaggerating their extent and importance and thereby of the United States being forced into matching with protective actions of its own. However, ignoring such policies could prove equally dangerous if, in fact, they proliferated until their impacts on the global trading system were severe.

Once the decision has been made to deal with these barriers, the lack of appropriate quantification presents new obstacles. Relevant data are needed to determine the significance of the removal of barriers and to define priorities. In the case of tariffs, reciprocal concessions could be roughly gauged, but quantifying the influence of nontariff barriers is much more difficult. It is possible to find numerous descriptions of the policies that governments implement to encourage investment, regional development, particular industries, and scientific research and technical development, and to promote exports. There are few studies, however, that estimate the quantitative importance of these benefits in determining trade performance.[36]

INDUSTRIAL ASSISTANCE: INFORMATION AGENCIES. The United States should take the lead in a concerted effort to remedy these deficiencies at

35. See Organization for Economic Cooperation and Development, *Transparency for Positive Adjustment: Identifying and Evaluating Government Intervention* (Paris: OECD, 1983).
36. See, however, Peter Morici and Laura L. Megna, *U.S. Economic Policies Affecting Industrial Trade: A Quantitative Assessment* (National Planning Association, 1983). For details on general patterns of federal assistance, see *Federal Support of U.S. Business* (Congressional Budget Office, January 1984).

both national and international levels. One way to launch such a global effort is as follows. In each country an independent analytical agency could be established and charged with the responsibilities of maintaining records and issuing reports on governmental assistance to industries and firms in all sectors of the economy for the purpose of bringing greater coherence to the totality of policies. Such reports would not only concentrate on measures explicitly linked to trade such as tariffs and quotas; they would also document other forms of assistance such as regional programs, effects of the tax system, and price-support programs. Whenever new measures were undertaken, the agency would estimate the costs and benefits and record the objectives as stated by policymakers. All policymaking bodies would be required to file information on policy actions to the agency. In subsequent years, the agency would evaluate the efficacy of such policies.

Such agencies may take different forms in different countries, depending on the particular institutional settings. It would be important that analysts most familiar with individual national circumstances be charged with compiling the data. However, data collection and methodology might be coordinated internationally to ultimately serve as the basis for negotiations. In the U.S. context ideally the agency would be an independent institution.

ANALYSIS, NOT POLICY. Currently there are several proposals to establish a U.S. council with representatives from business, labor, government, and the public to coordinate U.S. policy.[37] The goals of the information agency proposed here are different. Instead of allowing powerful interest groups to determine resource allocation, market forces would be enhanced by exposing the inconsistencies and inefficiency of government policies. Instead of allowing an unrepresentative political group to negotiate deals, an impartial body would provide recommendations to improve resource allocation. The agency proposed here might have industry advisory committees representing industry participants. It might also take testimony and hold hearings to ensure a broad consideration of views. But, ideally its findings would be determined by nonpartisan and impartial analysts.

37. Robert Reich, among others, has advocated enhancing the visibility of government industrial policy so that particular sectoral policies are based on public debate and on the participation of other industries, unions, and industry analysts. He advocates "a national bargaining arena for allocating the burdens and benefits of major adjustment strategies." Robert Reich, *The Next American Frontier* (New York Times Books, 1983), p. 276.

There are conceptual difficulties in measuring and quantifying the impact of various policies. In particular, cash outlays may not be the appropriate measure of subsidization. For example, with no budgetary outlays, government loan guarantees contain a grant element because they mean loans with lower interest than borrowers would otherwise obtain. Also there is no uniform method of calculating imputed transfers.[38] These difficulties are not insurmountable, however. Some industrial nations have already gathered data on all forms of industrial assistance (for example, the Federal Republic of Germany); others have provided comprehensive analysis of all forms of trade protection (the Australian Industries Assistance Commission). In the United States, estimates have been made of the size and effects of tariff and nontariff barriers across industries.[39] The U.S. treasury routinely provides extensive data on tax expenditures despite the absence of information on budgetary outlays.

To conclude, the agency proposed here would not be a panacea. Many structural policies reflect political pressures and not ignorance. Since efficiency is not the sole criterion for such policies, industrial assistance may be given despite costs. However, an estimate of the costs is surely a necessary first step for sound policy. With a clearer picture of the differential nature of the support for various industries, measures could be taken to remove the discrepancies in government industrial support. Such detargeting would strengthen the role of market forces in resource allocation.

Policies to Deal with Market Failure

There are a number of areas in which policy can be improved to address market failure. Some measures for improving the allocation of factors of production are outlined below.

38. For a discussion of these conceptual difficulties, see Seamus Cleireacain, "Measuring the International Effects of Subsidies," in Steven J. Warnecke, ed., *International Trade and Industrial Policies, Government Intervention, and an Open World Economy* (New York: Holmes & Meier, 1978), pp. 200–209. See also Alan R. Prest, *How Much Subsidy?* (London: Institute for Economic Affairs, 1975).

39. See, for example, Balassa and Balassa, "Industrial Protection in the Developed Countries"; Morici and Megna, *U.S. Economic Policies Affecting Industrial Trade: A Quantitative Assessment;* and Morris E. Morke and David G. Tarr, "Staff Report on Effects of Restrictions on United States Imports: Five Case Studies and Theory," prepared by the Federal Trade Commission, Bureau of Economics (U.S. Government Printing Office, June 1980).

Factors of Production

LABOR. Despite the profitability of investment in education, the private sector appears unwilling to provide unsecured loans to borrowers to finance their education and training. Since the government has superior means for ensuring repayment, there is a role for policy in facilitating such loans. Enrollment in certified educational and vocational institutions should qualify students to borrow the financial resources required to pay for their education. There is the danger that overly generous social provision for educational and retraining programs could result in abuse. Ensuring that ultimately users pay for such benefits would mitigate such perverse incentives. Loans could be made at market interest rates and, after graduation, collected by the Internal Revenue Service in tax returns. No one wishing to invest in themselves would be denied the opportunity through lack of funds. Some might balk at the idea of pricing such loans at market interest rates. What about students who are not as successful as they expected to be? The program could be adapted to meet such concerns by making the payments contingent upon future wage income. Within certain bounds, therefore, students would pay rates depending upon their income. The government could thus take a form of equity participation in the investment in human capital.[40]

One of the great strengths in the American economy is the flexibility of the labor market. But the U.S. system retains important structural impediments to change in both the workplace and the labor market. The impediments to upward mobility should be removed. For example, workers who leave their jobs often lose their pension rights. Legislation should make all pension plans vested in the individual rather than the job.

CAPITAL. The United States has attempted to increase investment by lowering corporate taxes, but this has been done in an essentially arbitrary and distorted manner. Because the accelerated cost recovery system is relatively more favorable to investment in equipment than in plant, industries for which short-lived equipment represents a large fraction of their total capital pay lower tax rates. The corporate income tax has become a relatively minor source of revenue but a major source of distortions in resource allocation.[41] The range of effective tax rates

40. Such a system is in operation at Yale University.
41. Auerbach estimates that in 1981 the social cost of the misallocation of capital within the U.S. corporate sector that resulted from differential asset taxation was equal

on industry has been increased substantially. For new investment, the range of effective tax rates has increased from 27.4 percent to 48.4 percent.[42] The biggest gainers are motor vehicles, transportation, petroleum refining, and mining. The biggest losers are utilities, services and trade, agriculture, machinery and instruments, and chemicals. Some of the firms penalized in the machinery, instruments, and chemical industries are high-technology operations with rapid growth potential. There are much simpler tax schemes that would facilitate the more rational distribution of capital across the various sectors of the economy. One of these would be to adopt a depreciation scheme under which the present value of all depreciation expenses could be immediately deducted.[43] Another scheme would be to allow business to deduct the entire cost of physical investments but not allow any deduction for interest payments or any investment tax credit.[44]

RESEARCH AND DEVELOPMENT. According to the National Science Foundation, from 1980 to 1983, real U.S. government support for nondefense R&D declined by 17 percent; support for basic research declined by 1.7 percent. This is inadvisable behavior for government in an economy in which productivity growth has declined. The difficulties of securing "property rights" to knowledge induce market failure. Knowledge is a classic public good in which additional application has no extra social costs. Once discovery is made, therefore, from a social standpoint knowledge should be freely available. But if firms cannot receive all social benefits, they may underinvest in knowledge creation. To improve the incentives for this knowledge creation, the government grants certain property rights through patents. The existence of patents and the ability to keep knowledge secret may also lead to a wasteful duplication of efforts to invent. Thus there are two types of problems: inadequate research in areas in which ownership of knowledge is difficult; and potentially excessive duplication of research in areas in which ownership is possible (through secrecy or property rights). These prob-

---

to 3.19 percent of the corporate capital stock. See Alan J. Auerbach, "Corporate Taxation in the United States," *Brookings Papers on Economic Activity, 2:1983*, pp. 451–513.

42. *Economic Report of the President, February 1982*, p. 124.

43. This was proposed in Alan J. Auerbach and Dale W. Jorgenson, "Inflation-Proof Depreciation of Assets," *Harvard Business Review* (September-October 1981), pp. 113–18.

44. See Paul N. Courant and Edward M. Gramlich, *Tax Reform: There Must Be a Better Way*, National Policy Exchange, no. 5 (November 1982), p. 28.

lems point to a strategy: direct social financial support for cases in which appropriation is a problem, and the removal of structural and legal obstacles to joint research for cases in which appropriation is possible.

The weakness in the free market in generating knowledge is related to the difficulty of retaining property rights to that knowledge. Basic science and generic types of research therefore warrant the most assistance. On the other hand, there is relatively less need for direct government intervention in commercial projects, where there are more possibilities for obtaining the rights. But there may be a role for improved coordination and for policies that facilitate joint research by commercial enterprises.

How should R&D be promoted? Simply subsidizing R&D indirectly through the tax code might not be an optimal response. Firms may use these tax breaks for wasteful effort that duplicates the products of rivals.[45] Despite tax breaks, firms may yet underinvest in knowledge that is difficult to appropriate. Thus a complex strategy is required. In addition to subsidizing private activities, the government might itself undertake research, fund it directly, or organize it through cooperative efforts among participants in the private or public sector. Nelson and Langlois summarize the findings of a series of case studies of U.S. policies toward R&D.[46] The approaches that they find have worked in the past are (1) support associated with government procurement or some other well-defined public-sector objective; (2) support of nonproprietary research with allocation of funds guided by the appropriate scientific community (for example, the National Science Foundation); and (3) provision of an institutional structure (such as the U.S. agricultural research system) that allows potential users to guide the allocation of R&D funds. But (4) where government has tried to "pick winners" in commercial competition, "the historical record seems unequivocally negative."

Government incentives should thus be general where government knowledge or expertise is lacking and specific where it has expertise.

45. Indeed, as Barry Bosworth notes, advertising firms have been the major recipients of R&D benefits from the 1981 tax code provisions. See Barry P. Bosworth, "Capital Formation, Technology, and Economic Policy," in *Industrial Change and Public Policy,* a symposium sponsored by the Federal Reserve Bank of Kansas City (FRB of Kansas City, 1983), pp. 231–66.

46. Richard R. Nelson and Richard N. Langlois, "Industrial Innovation Policy: Lessons from American History," *Science,* vol. 219 (February 18, 1983), pp. 817.

Government expertise and information are likely to be superior in areas in which the government itself is a major user of the research product. Thus government procurement programs may have an important and legitimate influence on R&D for national defense. The government can also provide financial stimulus but allow participants in the private sector and members of the research community to determine research where knowledge cannot be patented and has a broad public component. This is especially important in relatively competitive sectors such as agriculture in which private firms have difficulty in obtaining the full benefits of their research.

The government is much less able to intervene directly in developing technologies for commercial application. When there are gains external to the firm that can be captured by the industry, these can be realized by industry-wide ventures. The government should avoid hindering such activities. For example, U.S. semiconductor and computer firms, under the leadership of the Control Data Corporation, have formed the Microelectronic and Computer Technology to conduct long-term research in areas targeted by the Japanese. Antitrust difficulties will be avoided by having the results of this research licensed "at arms-length" to participating firms.[47]

Similarly, International Business Machines has been instrumental in creating the Semiconductor Research Corporation, which funnels R&D to selected universities for basic research in information-processing technology. Such activities, undertaken by consumers of the research, are more likely to be effective than research financed by the central government.

Not all R&D will ultimately benefit producers in the home country. Some discoveries may result in products made more cheaply abroad. The nature of R&D—that its results serve the public good—suggests encouraging an increased commitment to R&D around the world. Indeed, just as the burden of defense should be equitably divided among the allies, so the burden of undertaking basic scientific research should be similarly divided. Other nations should be encouraged to play a greater role in basic research. Foreign innovations raise U.S. consumers' living standards and increase the production options available to U.S. firms.

47. Edson W. Spencer, "Japan: Stimulus or Scapegoat," *Foreign Affairs*, vol. 62 (Fall 1983), pp. 131–37.

Regulating Firm Behavior

Major concerns are being raised about the need for reform in U.S. regulatory and antitrust policies. Much has been written about the unnecessary and burdensome government regulation that interferes with economic efficiency.[48] It need only be said that, to the degree that other governments do not similarly inhibit their firms, U.S. competitiveness suffers. This does not imply that the United States should not regulate, but simply that Americans should evaluate the costs.

The general point to be made about antitrust policy is that it can promote competitiveness of American industry as long as the appropriate market is kept in mind. Mistakes will be made if bigness per se is seen as an evil without recognition of the scale of an enterprise that is required to compete effectively in the world market. As is now acknowledged, in an open world economy U.S. industrial concentration ratios, as measured purely on a domestic basis, can be higher and larger than they could be if the United States were a closed economy. On the high-technology front this points to the greater tolerance now exhibited for cooperative ventures between American corporations in the development of new products. In the realm of declining industries, *provided markets are kept open,* rationalizations that reduce the number of U.S. firms should be permitted.

Concluding Observation: Limits to Policy

Some allegations about poor U.S. management practices may well be true. But changing these is not the responsibility of government. Government's role lies in ensuring that managers devote attention to satisfying their workers and their customers rather than to obtaining government aid or trying to minimize taxes.

It is often alleged that U.S. management decisionmaking horizons are too narrow both geographically and temporally and that U.S. managers are so preoccupied with financial and legal considerations that they

48. See Robert E. Litan and William D. Nordhaus, *Reforming Federal Regulation* (Yale University Press, 1983).

neglect the engineering and quality control aspects of production.[49] Frequently these U.S. flaws are contrasted with the Japanese prowess in management, worker discipline, and government industrial policy. Although widely accepted, these arguments may miss the point. By and large, attitudes and skills tend to be shaped by the environment. The alleged U.S. weaknesses may actually be strengths for an economy at the technological frontier operating in an uncertain environment. In contrast, the foreign adherence to long-range planning may better suit less-developed economies with clear schedules of changes in comparative advantage to follow and legacies of undervalued currencies. In an unstable world, it makes sense to maintain flexibility. U.S. economic growth has been much less steady than that of Japan.[50] In an economy with a higher proportion of declining industries, it makes sense to have more companies run by managers skilled in controlling costs or skilled in reallocating returns from "cash cows" to other industries.

It is somewhat ironic that as European economies approach U.S. income levels, some Europeans are looking to the United States as the appropriate management model. "We Europeans," a distinguished Scandinanvian banker says,

tend to stick to our long range plans come what may. We thus delay adjustments until the inventories pile up, the receivables are out of control and there is a severe liquidity bind. You Americans duck into the nearest doorway as soon as you feel one drop of rain. And since the Europeans, except for a handful of very big businesses, are still 20 years behind America in financial controls and information handling, we don't even know that the weather has changed until it's too late.[51]

49. Examples of these views can be found in Robert H. Hayes and William J. Abernathy, "Managing Our Way to Economic Decline," *Harvard Business Review,* vol. 58 (July-August 1980), pp. 67–77; Kim B. Clark, William J. Abernathy, and Alan M. Kantrow, "The New Industrial Competition," *Harvard Business Review,* vol. 59 (September-October 1981), pp. 68–79; and J. M. Juran, "Japanese and Western Quality: A Contrast in Methods and Results," *Sloan Management Review,* vol. 67 (November 1978), pp. 27–45.

50. As Trezise notes, "During more than two decades, 1951–1973, Japan had only one contraction of total output lasting as long as four quarters. Recessions, such as they were, typically were brief periods in which real GNP expanded at annual rates of 4 to 6 percent." Philip H. Trezise, "Industrial Policy in Japan," paper presented at the November 1983 meeting of the Southern Economic Association, p. 10.

51. Quoted by Peter F. Drucker, "Some High Marks for American Management," *Wall Street Journal,* August 17, 1981..

Similarly, Puri and Bhide note that in Japan,

Consensus smothers mavericks. Investments are made for the long haul but not for high returns and commensurate risks. Consensus may develop the best contract for a 20-year supply of iron ore, but decisions about where to drill for oil cannot be made by committee. That is the province of the Texas wildcatter.[52]

It will take a combination of both structural and macroeconomic policies to change U.S. attitudes. U.S. attitudes will change and institutions will and should become more likely to take the long-range view only after U.S. macroeconomic policies achieve greater stability, so that there is increased faith in steady economic growth.

The widespread provision of resources by the government creates unfortunate incentives—firms are induced to acquire rents from the government rather than profits from the market. The call for greater government intervention, on the grounds that it would make U.S. industry more farsighted, is ironic. For a world in which governments bail out private firms that fail to adapt is one that rewards myopic and static behavior. Even in a world in which some U.S. governmental response to actions of foreign governments is required, policymakers should not lose sight of what is the exception and what is the rule. The best rule for the United States is still to let the market allocate.

Postscript

This study analyzes U.S. manufacturing performance in a period that ends in 1982, when the U.S. economy was at the trough of a recession. A preliminary examination of the economic recovery in the United States between the end of 1982 and the time this book was published provides no reason to change its major conclusions. Overall the recovery has been quite normal; if anything, manufacturing output and employment growth have been stronger than might have been expected. The 6.2 percent growth in GNP between the fourth quarter of 1982 and the fourth quarter of 1983 was close to the average growth of 7.4 percent in the first year of five previous postwar recoveries. The 16.4 percent rise in manufacturing production during this 1982–83 period exceeded the

52. Tino Puri and Amar Bhide, "The Crucial Weaknesses of Japan Inc.," *Wall Street Journal*, June 8, 1981.

typical increase of 14.4 percent for manufacturing, while the 5 percent growth in manufacturing employment was equal to the average in previous expansions.

These numbers call into question suggestions that manufacturing unemployment had an unusually large structural component in the recession. Indeed, despite particularly weak performance in the foreign trade sector, the dimensions of both the recession and the recovery in manufacturing indicate the presence of an offsetting strength in the demand for manufactured goods within the domestic economy. Initially that demand came primarily from a large defense procurement; more recently it has also come from a spurt in equipment expenditures.

If the U.S. economy can grow at an annual average rate of 4 percent, the statistical evidence suggests that manufacturing employment in high-technology industries and in the rest of manufacturing will show average annual increases of 3.5 and 2.0 percent, respectively. If the dollar were to weaken, manufacturing employment growth could be even stronger.

There is an old story about the fool who was asked why he hit himself over the head with a hammer. His reply: because it feels so good when I stop. The removal of the self-inflicted wounds to U.S. manufacturing that stem from budgetary imbalances in the United States could have a similarly salutary effect on the American economy. If, over the next few years, U.S. policy could reduce the government deficit without curtailing investment incentives, the combination of strong domestic demand and a declining foreign exchange rate could result in extraordinary prosperity for American industry.

Classification Tables

Table A-1. *Categories for the Fifty-two Industries in U.S.*
Manufacturing, Based on the 1972 Input-Output Tables

Industry number	Category	Census SIC codes
13. Ordnance and accessories		3482–24, 3489, 3761, 3795
14. Food and kindred products		20
15. Tobacco manufactures		21
16. Broad and narrow fabrics, yarn, and thread mills		221–24, 226, 228
17. Miscellaneous textile goods and floor coverings		227, 229
18. Apparel		225
19. Miscellaneous fabricated textile products		239
20. Lumber and wood products, except containers		241–43, 2448, 249
21. Wood containers		2441, 2449
22. Household furniture		251
23. Other furniture and fixtures		252–54, 259
24. Paper and allied products, except containers and boxes		261–64, 266
25. Paperboard containers and boxes		265
26. Printing and publishing		27
27. Chemicals and selected chemical products		281, 286–87, 289
28. Plastics and synthetic materials		282
29. Drugs, cleaning and toilet preparations		283–84
30. Paints and allied products		285
31. Petroleum refining and related industries		29
32. Rubber and miscellaneous plastics products		30
33. Leather tanning and finishing		331
34. Footwear and other leather products		313–17, 319
35. Glass and glass products		321–23
36. Stone and clay products		324–29
37. Primary iron and steel manufacturing		331–32, 339, 3462
38. Primary nonferrous metals manufacturing		333–36, 3463
39. Metal containers		341
40. Heating, plumbing, and fabricated structural metal products		343–34
41. Screw machine products and stampings		345, 3465–66, 3469
42. Other fabricated metal products		342, 347, 349
43. Engines and turbines		351
44. Farm and garden machinery		352

146

Table A-1. *(continued)*

Industry number	Category	Census SIC codes
45.	Construction and mining machinery	3531–33
46.	Materials handling machinery and equipment	3534–37
47.	Metalworking machinery and equipment	354
48.	Special industry machinery and equipment	355
49.	General industry machinery and equipment	356
50.	Miscellaneous machinery, except electrical	359
51.	Office, computing, and accounting machines	357
52.	Service industry machines	358
53.	Electrical transmission and distribution equipment and industrial apparatus	361-62, 3825
54.	Household appliances	363
55.	Electric lighting and wiring equipment	364
56.	Radio, TV, and communication equipment	365–66
57.	Electronic components and accessories	367
58.	Miscellaneous electrical machinery, equipment, and supplies	369
59.	Motor vehicles and equipment	371
60.	Aircraft and parts	372
61.	Other transportation equipment	373–75, 3792, 3799, 2451
62.	Professional, scientific, and controlling instruments and supplies	381, 3822–24, 3829, 384, 387
63.	Optical, ophthalmic, and photographic equipment and supplies	383, 385–86
64.	Miscellaneous manufacturing	39

Source: *Survey of Current Business*, vol. 59 (February 1979), p. 54.

Table A-2. *Classification Scheme for the Fifty-two Input-Output Categories, by Production Characteristics and End Use*

End use	High-technology industries	Capital-intensive industries	Labor-intensive industries	Resource-intensive industries
Equipment	43. Engines and turbines		13. Ordnance and accessories	
	44. Farm and garden machinerey		23. Other furniture and fixtures	
	45. Construction and mining machinery		61. Other transportation equipment	
	46. Materials handling machinery and equipment			
	47. Metal working machinery and equipment			
	48. Special machinery			
	49. General industrial machinery			
	51. Office, computing, and accounting machines			
	52. Service industry machines			
	56. Radio and television equipment			
	60. Aircraft and parts			
	62. Scientific instruments			
Consumer durables	63. Optical equipment	54. Household appliances	19. Miscellaneous fabricated textiles	
			22. Household furniture	
			64. Miscellaneous manufacturing[a]	

Consumer
nondurables

29. Drugs, cleaning preparations

14. Food and kindred products
15. Tobacco

18. Apparel
34. Footwear
64. Miscellaneous manufacturing[a]

Intermediate
goods

27. Chemicals and selected chemical products
28. Plastics and synthetics
50. Miscellaneous machinery
53. Electrical and industrial equipment
55. Lighting equipment
57. Electrical components and accessories

16. Fabrics, yarn, thread
17. Miscellaneous textiles
25. Paperboard containers and boxes
26. Printing and publishing
30. Paints and allied products
32. Rubber products
35. Glass products
37. Iron and steel
39. Metal containers
41. Screw machine products
42. Other fabricated metal products

40. Heating and plumbing products
58. Miscellaneous electrical machinery, equipment, supplies
64. Miscellaneous manufacturing[a]

20. Lumber and wood products
21. Wood containers
24. Paper products
31. Petroleum refining and related industries
33. Leather products
36. Stone and clay
38. Nonferrous metals

Automobiles

59. Motor vehicles and equipment

Sources: Categories for production characteristics of industry are based on Robert M. Stern and Keith E. Maskus, "Determinants of the Structure of U.S. Foreign Trade, 1958–76," *Journal of International Economics*, vol. 11 (May 1981), pp. 207–24; end-use categories are taken from the 1976 revisions of industrial production by the Board of Governors of the Federal Reserve System. See *Survey of Current Business*, vol. 59 (February 1979), p. 54, for a complete description of the input-output categories.

a. The category "64. Miscellaneous manufacturing" is divided into end-use categories in the following proportions: consumer durables, 0.2; consumer nondurables, 0.4; and intermediate goods, 0.4.

Index

Abernathy, William J., 143n
Agriculture, 3, 18n, 111
Ahearn, Raymond J., 121n
Aho, C. Michael, 73n, 77n, 131n
Amacher, Ryan C., 119n
Antidumping laws, 113
Antitrust laws, 13–14, 89, 141, 142
Auerbach, Alan J., 139n
Automation, 2, 91
Automobile industry, 80n, 107, 128; employment, 9; legislation, 130; quotas on Japanese, 120; structural change, 55–61; technology, 79

Bagwhati, J., 131n
Baily, Martin Neil, 22n, 69n, 97n
Balassa, Bela, 74n, 120–21, 137n
Balassa, Carol, 120–21, 137n
Baldwin, Robert E., 42n, 119n, 120n, 123, 126
Banks: government development, 12; industrial policy, 106–07, 108
Baranson, Jack, 73n
Basiuk, Victor, 133n
Basu, S., 93n
Bayard, Thomas O. 131n
Belgium, 37
Bhide, Amar, 144n
Blackhurst, Richard, 43n
Bluestone, Barry, 51n
Bosworth, Barry P., 140n
Bowen, Harry P., 71n
Branson, William H., 71, 72n
Bushe, Dennis M., 43n
Business cycle, 89; declining employment, 81; demand, 69; manufactured goods trade, 45, 47

Canada, 6
Capacity utilization, 5
Capital: country without, 100; factor endowments, 71; factor supplies and growth, 21, 22; interest rates and inflows, 87;

structural policies, 138–39; trade policy, 106–07, 108
Capital formation, 4; comparing U.S. and foreign, 27–29
Capital stock: increase, 18–19, 22; shares in, 19–20
Carney, Richard D., 73n, 77n
Carter, Jimmy, 120
Clark, Kim B., 143n
Cleireacain, Seamus, 137n
Cline, William R., 121n
Competition, 12, 121; deficiencies of U.S. industrial system, 90; deindustrialization, 17; emergence of, 7–8, 91; erosion of price, 49–50; firm behavior, 142; foreign, 2; import, 97, 103, 125; interest rates, 88; legislation and automobile, 130; policy criteria, 101–04; productivity and, 3–4, 95; relative prices 38; short-run changes in U.S., 4
Computers, 3n, 141; employment, 9; technology, 79–80
Congress, 112, 119, 128
Cooper, Richard N., 123
Courant, Paul N., 139n
Currency, strength of dollar, 50, 87, 96

Dahrendorf, Rahl, 94n
Deardorff, Alan V., 127
Defense. *See* National defense
Deficits: government, 50, 87; trade, 94
Deindustrialization, 96; defining, 17–18; employment and, 41–43; extending analysis to *1980–82*, 44–45; relative prices and, 43; trade flows and, 43–44; U.S. position on, 92; value added and, 41–43
Demand, 4, 39, 40, 87; for automobiles, 55; income and substitution and, 69; for steel, 61; structural change and, 55, 67–69
Denzau, Arthur T., 110n
Deppler, Michael C., 43n
Destler, I. M., 120

151

156

Wages, 101
Warnecke, Stephen J., 123n, 137n
Weiss, Leonard, 121n
Willet, Thomas D., 119n

Williamson, Oliver E., 107n
Worker compensation, 131–32
Worker dislocation, 9–10
Workweek decline, 27